Capability of Elected Women Representatives on Gender Issues in Grassroots Governance

About the Author

Vanishree Joseph is currently working as Lecturer in the School of Gender and Development Studies, IGNOU, New Delhi. Previously she worked as Lecturer in Gandhigram Rural Institute—Deened University, Tamil Nadu. She has specialized in "Gender and Governance" in her doctoral programme. She is involved in organizing Panchayat Women Leaders for social development activities. She has received awards for her contribution in the forms of articles and presentations in the areas of gender and governance based on her field activities. She has written research articles in national and international journals and published monographs on the same area. To her credit she has three books as a co-author. She is in a network of scholars working in the field of capability approach.

Capability of Elected Women Representatives on Gender Issues in Grassroots Governance

Vanishree Joseph

CONCEPT PUBLISHING COMPANY PVT. LTD.
NEW DELHI-110059

ISBN-13: 978-81-8069-733-3

First Published 2011

Published and Printed by

Concept
Since 1974

Concept Publishing Company Pvt. Ltd.
Regd. Office:
A/15-16, Commercial Block, Mohan Garden
New Delhi-110059 (India)
Phones : 25351460, 25351794, *Fax* : 091-11-25357109
Email : publishing@conceptpub.com,
Website: www.conceptpub.com

Editorial Office:
H-13, Bali Nagar, New Delhi-110 015, India.

Cataloging in Publication Data--*Courtesy:* D.K. Agencies (P) Ltd. <docinfo@dkagencies.com>

Vanishree, J. (Joseph)
Capability of elected women representatives on gender issues in grassroots governance/ Vanishree Joseph.
p. cm.
Includes bibliographical references (p.) and index.
ISBN 9788180697333

1. Rural women--Political activity--India--Dindigul Anna (District) 2. Women in rural development--India--Dindigul Anna (District) 3. Panchayat--India--Dindigul Anna (District) 4. Feminism--India--Dindigul Anna (District) I. Title.

DDC 305.420954 22

Preface

This study aims to understand the functioning of elected women representatives of rural local governance on gender issues. Structural barriers in Indian society restrict women entering into political space. On their own women cannot enter the political arena and therefore reservations are needed to give them a chance to look into the factors which affect women and evolve a strategy which will change the condition and position of women. The opportunity afforded by the 33.3 per cent reservation of seats for women in rural local governance through the 73rd Constitutional Amendment Act in all the three-tiers of Panchayati Raj Institutions has widened the political space for rural women in India. Now the interaction between the women and governance draws attention as to how this political institution at the grassroots is going to affect women.

Firstly, this book analyses the freedom enjoyed by grassroots women leaders in the form of rights, opportunities and entitlements which enhance their capabilities in a male-dominated society. Secondly, the book tries to answer questions like will women perceive that the opportunity given to them is to address womens issues? Since it is expected that women can understand the problem of other women in a better way, will women come forward to address women issues through governance? The functioning of women representatives for the welfare and upliftment of women in their constituency can be termed as their agency functions. Will women leaders have the capability to make a substantial difference in women's life? Thirdly, the roles and responsibilities assigned to the grassroots leaders through the process of democratic decentralization, which aims at socio-economic political development was evaluated from the women's perspective.

To analyse these research problems Amartya Sen's "Capability Approach" was used as the analytical framework. Capability approach is a broad normative framework which evaluates the social arrangements and the extent of freedom people have to promote or achieve functionings they value. It examines what people are actually able to do. The range of alternatives they face while doing the function they value and to what extent they make decisions that matter to them. By using this framework the research was presented in two parts. The first part traces the instrumental factors which were measured in terms of freedoms classified by Amartya Sen as Political Freedom, Economic Facilities, Social Opportunities, Transparency Guarantees and Protective Security. These freedoms help in the formation of capabilities of Elected Women Representatives (EWRs) to perform their roles and responsibilities in the sphere of governance. In the second part, the acquired capabilities of EWRs were evaluated by analysing their functioning on women issues to perform agency functions.

This study was carried out in Dindigul District, one of the most backward districts in Tamil Nadu. The census survey was adapted in order to cover the entire study unit numbering 109 Elected Women Representatives of Village Panchayat. This research has adapted both quantitative and qualitative methods. An interview schedule was prepared based on the evolved indicators for freedom (independent variable) and functioning (dependent variable) of EWRs on women issues and administered with them. Further, to do qualitative analysis on freedom and functioning, case studies of EWRs were prepared. This book also gives policy recommendations to make considerable change in the Tamil Nadu Panchayats Act, 1994 and to institutionalize training for the EWRs.

The enormous expansion of women in decentralized governance structures has highlighted the advantage of proximity, namely the redress of grievance and most important of all, the ability to mobilize struggle at a local level where it is most meaningful. The vast differences in the role assigned to them by the Tamil Nadu Panchayat Act 1994, and the role assumed by them for the welfare of women folk in particular manifests their preference of action and commitment towards the society. In the villages, women begin to see themselves as more than mothers and wives, and become active members of the Panchayat. But when women lack freedom it amounts to deprivation of women's active agency. But it is also the case that the limited role of women's active agency seriously afflicts the lives of all people. While there is every reason not to slacken the concern about women's well-being and ill-being, and to continue to pay attention to the sufferings and deprivations of women, there is also an urgent and basic necessity, particularly at this time, to take an agent oriented approach to women's agenda.

The study shows that indicators of women's agency range from raising consciousness of women's issues to changing institutional structures and process and influencing the governance discourse itself. Even though the expectations on women politicians are higher, they do not necessarily do so and cannot, because they do not have equal access and control with men to the means for political participation. Moreover, the powers and functions entrusted to them in local governance are not much significant to operate women's agenda. Also they face numerous problems when they are in power. The study also pinpoints that instead of tackling the problems of women, the women representatives have started facing a multitude of problems.

The continued absence of women's voice in governance now draws the policy makers' attention and women tend to assert themselves and have started claiming their rights. Still due consideration is yet to be given. Much more still needs to be done. Women should be capacitated in such a way that they directly influence the broader political and economic measures. Constraints on women within family and society have a direct impact on their capability for public engagements. Suitable measures should be taken to eradicate these constraints and a conducive atmosphere should be created for women to perform agency function in the public domain.

J. Vanishree

Acknowledgements

I would like to express my deepest sense of gratitude to my guru and research supervisor, Dr.G.Palanithurai, Professor, Department of Political Science and Development Administration, Gandhigram Rural University. His intellectual guidance and encouragement have made it possible for me to sail through this study. I must also record my gratefulness to Dr.C.Sivaprakasam, and Mr. S. P. Ramesh for their technical support to complete this study. My friend Dr. G. Uma has helped me to finetune my interview schedule and also made arrangements for the data collection. I would like to take this opportunity to express my thanks to her. Prof. M. A. Jayaraju helped me in polishing my language style. I acknowledge his help extended to me. I am extremely indebted to the women Village Panchayat Presidents of this study. Without their support this study would not have been possible. They have been extremely patient and helpful in answering my questions. Finally, I record my heartfelt thankfulness to my parents for their encouragement and unflinching support throughout my work.

J. Vanishree

Contents

List of Tables

List of Figures

List of Abbreviations

AIDS	-	Acquired Immune Deficiency Syndrome
CBO	-	Community Based Organisation
DRDA	-	District Rural Development Agency
EWRs	-	Elected Women Representatives
FC	-	Forward Community
FIR	-	First Information Report
GDI	-	Gender Development Index
GEI	-	Gender Equality Index
GO	-	Government Order
HDI	-	Human Development Index
HDR	-	Human Development Report
HDRC	-	Human Development Resource Centre
MBC	-	Most Backward Community
MLA	-	Member of Legislative Assembly
MP	-	Member of Parliament
NFHS	-	National Family Health Survey
NGO	-	Non-Governmental Organisation
PRI	-	Panchayati Raj Institutions
RD	-	Rural Development
SC	-	Scheduled Caste
SHG	-	Self-Help Group
ST	-	Scheduled Tribes
TASMAC	-	Tamil Nadu State Marketing Corporation Ltd
UN	-	United Nations
UNDP	-	United Nations Development Programme
WDP	-	Women's Development Programme

1

Introduction

The status of women in India can be assessed by quantifying the rate of female infanticide, foeticide, abduction, dowry death, torture, molestation, sexual harassment, unequal inheritance and property rights, desertion, polygamy etc. The persistence of sharp gender inequalities in many different forms is one of the most striking aspects of Indian society, and it yields disparities in well-being as well as differences in power and decision-making authority.[1] The different focus of gender inequality[2] can be stated as:

1. Survival inequality,
2. Natality inequality,
3. Unequal facilities,
4. Ownership inequality,
5. Unequal sharing of household benefits and chores, and
6. Domestic violence and physical victimization.

The UNDP's[3] Human Development Report 2006 (UNDP) shows that India ranks 97 in gender related development index. The adult literacy rate of females is 47.8 per cent while for males it is 73.4 . The estimated earned income of (PPP US$) females is only 1,442 whereas for males it is 3,820 but the work burden of females is higher than that of males. Women work for 457 minutes per day and men work for 391 minutes only. Further, a woman allocates 65 per cent of time for non-market activities while men spend only 8 per cent of time for the same. In spite of all her work burden and time allocation, the value of her work is underestimated and in turn she earns less compared to men. Apart from this, the condition of women is worse regarding health. It is noted by the National Family Health Survey-2 that 51.8 per cent of married women between the ages of 15 and 49 have anemia, and nutritional anemia caused by iron deficiency contributes to 19 per cent of maternal deaths. Women's status is comparatively lower than men's while women constitute half of the population of the country. Third World women are often portrayed as generally poor, illiterate and ignorant. Their unequal economic and social status, low literacy level, poor health, high maternal mortality and disadvantages under the law stem from their lack of participation in development.

The democratic decentralization process in India along with the provision for women to hold and participate in decision-making positions is a good start to improving the status of women in India. One of the significant goals set by the Fourth World Conference on Women in Beijing was adequate representation for women in all decision-making bodies. It was suggested that in any representative body there should be a logical balance of men and women to voice the concerns of the society en masse. Mahbub ul Huq, the pioneer of human development approach, states that, "Local bodies, if properly utilized can be vehicle of women's active participation when it is effectively mainstreamed. Since these institutions function at the grassroots level, representatives, both men and women, are more aware of, and can be more responsive to the needs of women and children as well as to the problems of rural communities. Tapping into the latent capacity of women is essential to substantially enhancing the socio-economic development of South Asia. Decentralization is thus a pre-requisite for effective mainstreaming of women's concern in development".[4]

The on-going process of democratic decentralization coupled with the concept of women's participation in governance is expected to create a significant impact on the development of India. One of the important reasons why women have not received adequate benefits from years of planning and development is their inadequate representation, non-participation and non-involvement in the preparation and execution of plans for their economic development and social justice through decentralized institutions.[5] The opportunity provided through the reservation of seats for women in local governance through the 73rd and the 74th Constitutional Amendment Acts also represents a call for solving gender issues in the society. Women's insights and values of governance can find means and measures to solve the problem of gender inequality. Further, rural women, who are the majority in the population of women in India, easily succumb to the features of patriarchy and are deprived of a decent standard of living.

The opportunity through 33.3 per cent reservation of seats in rural local governance has been created in all the three tiers of Panchayati Raj Institutions and among these three tiers the village panchayat occupies a predominant position where rural people have access to the process of governance directly and also where concepts like participation, transparency and accountability become operationalised. Here the representatives' proximity to the people, makes them to understand the problems of the people better. The problem of women can be better articulated and finds better solution only by women, and the presence of grassroot governance has provided an ample scope for women representatives to focus on gender issues. Against this backdrop, it is proposed to undertake a study to analyse the role of Elected Women Representatives (EWRs) on the issues of gender, which affect the life of women at the grassroots.

Statement of the Problem

In a traditional, highly backward, feudal, patriarchal and hierarchical social structure access to positions of decision-making in the public domain are restricted to men of particular families and castes. Further, women across the world are subordinated and politically under-represented. Structural barriers in the society also restrict women from entering into the political space. To ensure that women are not isolated in political life different strategies have been used to increase their representation and one among them is the reservation of seats in the political space. Women on their own cannot enter the political arena and therefore reservations are needed to give them a chance to look into the factors which affect women and evolve a strategy which will change the condition and position of women at present. As more women occupy political space, they are expected to change the agenda of politics. By attaining a critical mass of women, the political norms and the political culture can be changed. Women are then able to choose to act as individuals or with specific women's or feminist point of view.[6]

The 73rd amendment to the Constitution of India and the provision of 33.3 per cent reservation of seats has facilitated the election of one million women to decision-making positions in rural local bodies.

The process of democratic decentralization in India, which is pro-women also, is expected to create a significant change in the lives of women. The process of empowering women on the one hand and the social, political, economic and religio-cultural dimensions of society on the other, will certainly influence women's position in power. Now, the interaction between women and governance draws attention as to how this political institution at the grassroots is going to affect women. The capability of women to play an influential role in local politics and decision-making is put under scrutiny. Two major factors have to be analysed. One is the prolonged prevalence of male supremacy over females which has its own impact on the freedom enjoyed by the latter and the other is the roles and responsibilities entrusted to them through the process of decentralized local governance.

First, the sexual hierarchical society, placing man at the apex, won't allow women to exercise political power. So the power given to them will be challenged on most occasions. When power is reserved for women in a male dominated society, it becomes imperative to analyse the freedom enjoyed by those women in the form of rights, opportunities and entitlements which enhances their capabilities. Will these women in power have political freedom, economic facilities, social opportunities, transparency guarantees and protective security to perform their roles and responsibilities?

The second problem lies in the perception of women who have been subordinated and suppressed from their birth through the process of socialization. It is important to know that those who fill the seats are aware of the problems that women face and are interested in creating change within the community. Will the women perceive that the opportunity given to them is to address gender issues? Will the women come forward to address the problem through governance? Will women leaders have the capability to make a 'substantial difference' in women's life?

Third, the roles and responsibilities assigned to the grassroots leaders through the process of democratic decentralization, which aims at socio-economic political development, should be evaluated from the women's perspective. Will this power structure in the form of decentralized governance provide ample scope for the welfare of women?

At this juncture, it is essential to look at whether women in local governance have the capability to perceive the problem of their fellow beings; whether they have the freedom to exercise their political power; whether women in local governance will perform on the issues of gender; whether women in local governance have the capability to influence the process of governance in favour of women to bring about substantial change. It is with these questions that the present study has been undertaken to examine the capability of elected women representatives in grassroots governance on gender issues.

Review of Literature

The available literature on women, governance and gender issues provides a conceptual framework for analysing the freedom enjoyed and functioning by elected women representatives in grassroots governance on gender issues. The literature can be classified under three broad groups, viz., conceptual review, theoretical review and empirical review.

Conceptual Review

The conceptual review helps to understand concepts like decentralization, gender and governance used in the present context.

G. Palanithurai's[7] *Grassroots Democracy in Indian Society* analyses the present scenario of governance in India and its implications for the society from the perspective of people's participation in the process of development. It is a collection of essays touching upon a wide variety of subjects, namely, election, governance, people's participation, development, devolution of powers, reconstruction of the political structure, planning exercise done by the people, food security and building the capacity of the people and their leaders at the grassroots. It focuses mainly on the positive aspects of the devolution of powers and people's participation in the process of economic development and social justice.

D. Bandyopadhyay's[8] *Gender and Governance in India* describes the Indian State's response to the oppression of women as hypocritical at its worst and schizophrenic at its best. He states that women in our society suffer from a double jeopardy. Under an iniquitous and unequal socio-economic order which promotes and sanctifies exploitation and oppression, both vulnerable men and women suffer. Moreover as an effect and concomitant attribute of this irrational and unethical order, women suffer greater subordination and deprivation both at home and in society. He also criticizes the Government of India for not taking any action at any point of the Beijing Platform of Action.

Wandana Sonalkar's[9] *An Agenda for Gender Politics* analyses the two issues of gender politics which are currently being debated—first reservation for women in Parliament and state legislatures, and second, the on-going debate over the Uniform Civil Code. She says that patriarchy in India starts with the control of women or men in the family but works in such a way as to perpetuate caste hierarchies, and the preservation of caste is the basis for the functioning of this patriarchy. And she questions whether the passage of the Women's Reservation Bill as it is, as a first measure, without a wide-ranging discussion of the underlying caste issues really empowers women in the struggle against patriarchy in the social and political specificity of present day India.

Farida Vahedi[10] in her article "Gender Equality and Social Responsibility" explains that the progress of humanity depends on men and women working together—both must be equally developed. Women, given equal opportunities for education, have already proved to be the equals of men in intellectual and creative capacity. Men must encourage and facilitate the full development of women, as women must support men in their development towards this new condition of society. The transition to full equality between women and men is an evolutionary process requiring education and patience with oneself and others, as well as an unswerving determination.

Shobhita Rajagopal and Kanchan Mathur[11] in their article "Women's Empowerment through State Benevolence" explain the experience of Rajasthan. Rajasthan was one of the first states to launch a participatory and innovative Women's Development Programme (WDP) which was successful enough to challenge the socio-political power structures and was in time, derailed. A major criticism of the policy came from women's groups. According to them, contrary to the statements made by the state officials, neither their views nor the interests of grassroots women were taken into consideration at the time of policy formulation. Women's gender interests cannot be conceived in an abstract and universal manner. They have to be contextualized and seen as an element in a continuing process of identity formation and political conscientisation.

B. Suguna[12] in her article "Women's Empowerment: Concept and Framework" explains the process of empowerment. It has provided a broad-based activity schedule to the national, regional and global agencies in which participation has been highlighted. By this method, participation of women in the decision-making process could be enhanced many-fold and progress attained in a much shorter time. The process of empowerment helps in identifying areas to be targeted, planning strategies for action and outcomes. Empowerment is not a process which is horizontal or vertical, but a process which goes in a circle. Here the beginning ends in change and the change leads to another beginning. No one magic formula can exist for empowerment. It has to be tailor made to suit the clients.

Vina Mazumdar[13] in her article "Women: From Equality to Empowerment" explains the background of women's movement in India and analyses the measures taken by the Indian state for gender justice. Women's empowerment like 'National Integration'—a phrase which has done more damage to the Indian polity than any provisions for reservation—is historically linked with (a) the 'Sanskritization process'—which 50 years of 'modernization' operating 'democratically' has not been able to weaken (and which globalization has only enhanced and accelerated); and (b) development of new social institutions and values which can challenge social hierarchy, patriarchy and the politics of accidents of birth buttressing the theory of purity-pollution, which has always haunted our history. It is time for India to try out some new experiments in achieving real democracy, and provide some new basis for the formation of political identities. The Indian Women's Movement could offer many suggestions and opportunities for both.

Indhrani Sridharan's[14] article "Practicing Human Rights: A Feminist Perspective" discusses the issues concerning women which are not given priority in society. It is a wrong notion that women have to fight men in order to obtain their rights. The issue should be presented as a joint struggle for change in society. In a society where definitions, policies and rules are male-oriented, the need is to understand woman and her rightful place in society. Her role and contribution has become not only a necessity, but also a base on which the new society and civilization are being reconstructed. It is time to go beyond ideology and theory into the world of praxis, a world of greater hardship for women, who sacrifice their identity, communication and hopes, in a society dominated by male values. What is needed in addition is the recognition of women's equal humanity and a continuing response to the persistent realities of the contemporary world. The right of every individual is to do what he or she values: and becoming and being human is always more difficult for a woman.

Shobna Sonpar and Ravi Kapur[15] in their article "Non-Conventional Indicators: Gender Disparities under Structural Reforms" explain the prevalence of mental distress and of abuse and violence are important indicators of the well-being of a community and are significantly differentiated by gender. The socio-economic changes brought about by structural reforms have the potential to disrupt existing notions of gender in ways that could be threatening, demoralizing and oppressive for men and women in some contexts and empowering in others. Some of these factors, especially those that concern gender, ideology, may indeed be difficult to measure. It is therefore necessary to consider research methodologies that go beyond the quantitative in order to do justice to the complexity of these phenomena.

Nirmala Buch[16] in her paper "Women's Experience in New Panchayats: The Emerging Leadership of Rural Women" presents some of the findings of her study on women's representation and participation in Panchayats. She recaptures the steps taken in India from time-to-time for the revitalization of Panchayats. In the second part she presents the evolution of representation for women in these institutions in colonial and post-colonial India. The findings of the study discuss women in Panchayats after the amendment in 1992 mandating a minimum one-third representation to women in all Panchayats in the country. The study captures their experience and impact in three northern states of Madhya Pradesh, Rajasthan and Uttar Pradesh. The study explores various aspects, including the newly elected women's socio-economic profile, motivation to enter these institutions, awareness and knowledge, participation, performance, constraints, aspirations, support of various social institutions and the community members' perception of their impact and performance.

Jennie Litvack, Junaid Ahmad and Richard Bird[17] in their paper "Rethinking Decentralization in Developing Countries" explain the reasons for decentralization and the dimensions of decentralization. It also helps us to understand the factors which affect the ideal and the actual form of decentralization.

Kamla Bhasin[18] in her book *Understanding Gender* explains the concept of gender and in the process of gendering how culture has its ways of valuing girls and boys and assigning them different roles, responses and attributes. She tries to say that neither sex nor nature is responsible for the unjustifiable inequalities that exist between women and men. Like the inequalities between castes, classes and races, these too are man-made; they are historical constructs and therefore they can be questioned, challenged and changed. A woman may well have children but that should be no reason for her inferiority and subordination; nor should it determine her education, training or job opportunities. She also explains the need for a change from Women in Development to Gender and Development approach where it was pointed out that to improve women's condition and status and to make them partners in development, it is essential to understand the causes of women's subordination, to examine the social system (patriarchy) which keeps women oppressed and subordinated.

B.K. Nagla[19] in her article "Sex and Gender: Cognitive Analysis" tries to look at the history of feminist theorizing that leads to three kinds of essentialism of women: (1) Relationship between the concepts of sex and gender, (2) The structure of particular culture and societies in shaping the identities of women, and (3) Identity crisis of feminism. All these three types of essentialism refer to a form of reductionism. They are associated with a similar problem of identity: the primary interest is to explore the ways in which gender has been analysed in feminist theories and to investigate how these conceptions bear upon issues of female empowerment. The idea behind this paper, briefly, is first to define the concept of gender, and then to examine the structure and culture of societies in order to understand the identity crisis of feminism.

Naila Kabeer[20] in her book *Reversed Realities: Gender Hierarchies in Development Thought* analyses different approaches to development of women and explains gender and power in social sciences. She describes the radical view which distinguishes between three different interpretations of Lukes's power, commonly found in the social science literature. "The Power To", is closely associated with liberal forms of analysis and is concerned with decision-making on issues over which there is an observable conflict. "The Power Over" inheres in the implicitly accepted and undisputed procedures within institutions which, by demarcating decisionable from non-decisionable issues, systematically and routinely benefit certain individuals and groups at the expense of others. The third dimension of power assumes that conflicts of interest may be suppressed not only from the decision-making agenda, but also from the consciousness of the various parties involved. The multi-dimensional nature of power suggests that empowerment strategies for women must build on "The Power Within" as a necessary adjunct to improving their ability to control resources, to determine agendas and to make decisions.

Asha Ramesh and Bharti Ali[21] in their book *33.3 per cent Reservation Towards Political Empowerment* analyse whether the decentralized system of governance can create a conducive environment for women and other weaker sections to perform effectively or not. Over one million women have currently entered the political arena. While this affirmative action has brought women into decision-making positions, neither are supportive mechanisms introduced, nor is the prevailing social climate conducive to facilitate this process. In this book an attempt has been made to examine in-depth all the above aspects with the thrust being on what impedes or promotes women's political participation. They also suggest that to enable women take on the political challenge, several affirmative initiatives need to be taken like education, awareness and information, training, gender sensitization programmes and changes in the law and rules governing panchayats/municipal bodies.

Martha C.Nussbaum[22] in her book *Human Capabilities: Women, Culture and Development* explains that development starts and ends with people. For a country's advancement, nothing is stronger, richer and more generative than human resource. The capability approach deals with the capabilities and needs that join all humans' share and not those which enhance the power and status of any dominant group. Capability is a substantive freedom to achieve alternative functioning combinations—less formally the freedom to achieve various possible life styles. To assess the gender inequality she has also selected capabilities like life and physical health, mental well-being, bodily integrity and safety, social relations, political empowerment, education and knowledge, domestic work and non-market care, paid work and other projects, shelter and environment, mobility, leisure activity, time autonomy, respect and religion.

Jean Dreze and Amartya Sen[23] in their book *India: Development and Participation* discuss women's agency and change. The agency of women is effective in promoting goals which women tend to value. When those values are distorted by centuries of inequality, for example yielding the perception that boys are to be welcomed more than girls, then the empowerment of women can go hand in hand with persistent inequality and discrimination in some fields, in particular 'boy preference' in births. Indeed, the agency of women can never be adequately free if traditionally discriminatory values remain unexamined and unsecrutinized. While values may be culturally influenced, it is possible to overcome the barriers of inequality imposed by tradition through greater freedom to question, doubt and—if convinced—reject. An adequate realization of women's agency relates not only to the freedom to act but also to the freedom to question and reassess. Critical agency is a great ally of development.

Anupama Roy[24] in "Community, Women Citizens and a Women's Politics" argues that the articulation of women as 'citizens in India was intricate within a web of discourses of liberation and equality which made the national-political and religious-cultural communities, the primary, and often contesting sources of a person's identity as citizen. The primacy given to community membership, and the manner in which women were implicated in it, has had important ramifications on voicing women as citizens and on carving out a space for 'women's' politics.

Karunakar Patnaik[25] in his article "Devolution of Powers to Panchayati Raj Institutions in India: An Overview" says devolution of powers and transfer of subjects to the Panchayati Raj Institutions should not be made either a political gimmick or election rhetoric. It shall be prudent for the MPs and MLAs including ministers and the bureaucracy to consider transfer of powers to Panchayati Raj Institutions in India as mandatory and duty bound with grace and humility. A system cannot die of power. It can die of a death in attitude.

Rehana Ghadially's[26] edited volume on *Women in Indian Society* provides coherent analyses and fresh perspectives concerning the issues and problems that affect women's lives in India. The book is divided into five sections which cover (a) contextual, analytical and theoretical views of women; (b) empirical research organized around existing stereotypes about men and women; (c) an exploration of common forms of violence against women; (d) the way women are portrayed in diverse media; and, (e) a description of the growing efforts to sensitize people to the inequalities between the sexes. Demographic factors, marginalizing of women in the developmental process and oppressive social reality highlight the miserable plight of women and the long struggle ahead of them. Awareness of inequality and oppressiveness is a precondition to any kind of social change. While consciousness-raising groups have often been described as the hallmark of new feminism in the west, sustained activity in a variety of fields by autonomous women's groups has been the prime generator of greater social awareness about women's problems in India.

A.M. Shah, B.S. Baviskar and E.A. Ramaswamy[27] in their edited book *Social Structure and Change: Women in Indian Society* focus on the changing status of women in Indian society. Based on primary as well as secondary data, these cogently argued essays provide a valuable framework to assess the process of reform and change in Indian society within a gender perspective. Moving beyond the usual internalist and externalist approaches to the gender question, the discussion focuses on the interplay between the familial domain and the external forces that impinge on it. Various essays explore issues related to the survival and the nurturance of the girl child, her access to education and participation in productive activity and, most importantly, her right to natal property. This discussion is located in the context of external developments such as improved irrigation and the commercialization of agriculture, shifts in land ownership patterns and the dynamics of caste affiliations.

In his article, "Indian Democracy and Empowerment of Women", J.P. Singh[28] asserts that neither male domination nor the state has been really opposed to democratic rights of women, as is the case even in the developed world. To him, India's record has been both laudable and favourable for women. Discussing a two-pronged strategy of women empowerment—i.e., political, through the Bill seeking reservation of seats in legislatures; and economic, through economic development programmes—in the present context, he, however, argues in favour of economic empowerment through affirmative action rather than adopting a gender-based reservation at union, state, or local levels.

Carol le Bacchi's[29] book *The Politics of Affirmative Action* draws upon current social and feminist theory to present a lucid analysis of the implementation of reform. Taking account of the particular historical context of affirmative action policies, she considers why expressed commitment to affirmative action for women has failed to translate into meaningful reform. She describes how conceptual and identity categories are given meanings and positioned in debate in ways which work to contain the effects of the reform. Bacchi concludes that proponents of affirmative action need to direct more attention to the political uses of categories rather than to their abstract content, and to concentrate their efforts upon exposing the effectives of category politics.

Maitrayee Mukhopadhyay[30] in her article "On Creating Citizens Who Demand Just Governance: Gender and Development in the

Twenty-First Century" discusses the issue of good governance and global development in the 1990s. By and large, this translated into policies aimed at build accountability of public administration institutions to the broad 'public', but omitted to consider two issues: first, the 'public' consists of women and men, who have gender—differentiated needs and interests; second, civil society institutions have a role to play in creating the demand for democratic, accountable, and just governance. To address these omissions, and to reinforce the importance of bringing a gender perspective to global debates and approaches to international development, at the Royal Tropical Institute in Amsterdam, initiated a three-year programme in 1999. It is entitled 'Gender, Citizenship, and Governance'. This article discusses the programme and its relevance to international development, and provides three case studies from the programme; from India, Bangladesh, and South Africa.

The UNDP's[31] essays on *Gender and Governance* says that the relationship between gender and governance has too often been neglected in both theoretical and empirical work. These papers aim to set the record straight. They advance a theoretical structure, both positive and normative, within which the question of gendered governance may usefully be pursued. They also analyse some current developments that indicate many ways in which women are actively participating in governance, in both government and the institutions of civil society, and the obstacles that remain. These papers use normative concepts such as "development", "human development", "progress", and "improvement". The use of such normative notions is inevitable and deeply right in academic work aimed at pointing out productive directions for social intervention.

The document on "Decentralization in India: Challenges and Opportunities" prepared by the HDRC[32] attempts to articulate the connection between economic dependency of vulnerable groups on the local elite on the one hand and the effectiveness of local governance institutions in delivering basic services to the poor on the other. In brief, in order to transform present realities, it is imperative to strengthen decentralization from below, so that the voices of the poor can carry weight in village assemblies and ward council meetings. Apart from social mobilization, this can be accomplished by strengthening community networks and institutions. Initiatives that empower the poor, especially women, to manage local resources and local institutions are steps in this direction. The success of the world's largest experiment in deepening democracy ultimately depends upon the success of these initiatives.

The UNDP's[33] document on "Women's Political Participation and Good Governance: 21st Century Challenges" highlights a close relationship between the low number of women parliamentarians and the high number of women in poverty. It also underscores that the budget of any nation is the most important economic instrument for improving the well-being of its citizens. The marginalization of women in the political process and governance in general has been both the cause and the effect of the slow progress made in the advancement of women.

Kamla Bhasin's[34] *What is Patriarchy?* is a conceptual work on the nature, origin and roots of patriarchy in South Asia. It helps to understand the situation better. Generally speaking a large number of women's groups in South Asia seem to accept the Socialist Feminist Position, i.e., that both patriarchy and class oppression are important, are related to, and in most cases, reinforce each other, and that women have to simultaneously challenge the system of patriarchy and class and caste domination.

Kamla Bhasin and Nighat Said Khan[35] in their book—*Some Questions on Feminism and Its Relevance in South Asia* explain what is feminism and find that feminism is not only necessary for our society but also very exciting for all those who are participating in the process of defining, articulating, shaping and living it. Feminism is exciting precisely because it is challenging us into reviewing, redefining and changing the most intimate of relationships, the most personal of beliefs, the most unarticulated areas of our minds and hearts.

The publication "Local to Local Dialogue: A Grassroots Women's Perspective on Good Governance"[36] describes locally designed strategies through which grassroots women's groups initiate and engage in on-going dialogue with local authorities, with a view to influencing policies, plans and programmes in ways that address women's priorities. The six case studies chronicle the experiences and efforts of each of the women's groups to identify priorities and negotiate with local authorities and in some cases other government authorities.

Emma Bell's[37] "Emerging Issues in Gender and Development: An Overview" provides a brief overview of the emerging issues in gender and development policy, practice and theory. This report on emerging issues starts by exploring sector-wise approaches (SWAps) and the extent to which they have enabled the integration of gender equality concerns. SWAps are increasingly being adopted by donor agencies as an effective and efficient way to ensure that development initiatives have national reach and ownership.

Stephanie Tawa Lama-Rewal's[38] article "Fluctuating, Ambivalent Legitimacy of Gender as a Political Category" discusses the debate over the Women's Reservation Bill. Debates around the Women's Reservation Bill, whatever their particular stance, have all taken for granted the legitimacy of gender as a political category, in contrast to the fierce controversy that the issue provoked in France in the 1990s over the same issue of political representation of women. With this as a starting point for a reflection on the status of gender in the Indian polity, the author explores the historical fluctuations of gender's legitimacy as a political category, the principles on which this legitimacy is founded and, lastly, its intrinsic ambivalence.

Esther Duflo's[39] *Why Political Reservations?* assesses the case for reservations. Several countries have introduced procedures—either explicit quotas or forms of gerrymandering—to ensure political representation for disadvantaged groups, such as women or ethnic minorities. In India, seats are reserved for historically disadvantaged groups and women at all levels of the Panchayat system. On the basis of the evidence accumulated about the Indian experience, this paper reviews the case for reservations.

James Manor[40] in his '*Political Economy of Democratic Decentralization*' clearly defines decentralization and explains the diverse causes for the necessity of decentralized democracy in various parts of the world. He also explores the ideas concerning decentralization and relations of politics, state-society with decentralization. To make it successful he suggests that sufficient powers, financial resources, adequate administrative capacity and reliable accountable mechanism must vest with decentralized institutions.

Bidyut Mohanty and Shashi Narayana[41] have edited a book on *Women and Political Empowerment 2001*. It was an edited document of the women's political Empowerment Day celebrations at a time when the Government of India had declared 2001 as Women's Empowerment Year. This provided a forum for elected women representatives, academics, human rights activists, members of voluntary agencies to discuss women's political empowerment making an impact on related issues like primary health care, primary education, family welfare, poverty eradication and economic empowerment. The issues that emerged during the discussions were whether political empowerment would automatically lead to economic empowerment or *vice-versa*. A consensus was reached that both these aspects are complementary to each other for creating an enabling environment. Education, awareness and the presence of a strong women's movement also contribute substantially towards women's political and economic empowerment.

Theoretical Review

The theoretical review helps to spell out the theoretical relationship between gender and governance.

Kumud Sharma[42] in her article "Institutionalizing Feminist Agenda(s)" states that the practices of the women's movement are continually being transformed to meet new challenges. Yet feminist politics is constantly confronted by a skepticism against institutionalized politics; it displays an uneasiness with the forms of power that dominate political processes. Similarly the politics of mainstreaming women's studies implies that feminist scholarship has had to cope with the complex web relationships within academia dominated by a patriarchal academy and knowledge hierarchy. But, as this paper explains, while institutional locations may also form their own sites of contest, the need for a renewed and sustained struggle from such locations, employing new interventions in the hope of transforming institutions, remains of crucial importance for the women's movement.

Maitreyi Krishnaraj[43] in her article "Challenges before Women's Movement in a Changing Context" argues that communalism, the actual and possible effects of economic reforms on women's position, and the rising violence in our society have become problematic issues for the women's movement. Many of these developments have roots in the past while some are new emanations. The feminist response to these issues has been more in the form of a generalized anxiety rather than clear analysis and understanding of the nature of our polity and changes therein; the nature of economic reforms and how they have been carried out; policy shifts in many areas and their impact on different sections of women and, importantly, where the movement's energies should be spent. The author also states that research agendas must move to studies at greater depth and debates on public issues must once again find women taking active part.

Vinay Bahl's[44] article on "What Went Wrong with History from Below?" states that recent academic debates on theoretical dichotomies have obscured several crucial issues such as emancipation and social justice. For those writing history from below, new dilemmas present themselves, as conservatism, feeding on such reinterpretation, presents itself with a new legitimacy while spontaneous efforts to empower people have ended up being co-opted within the prevailing political system. To bring back emancipatory politics and social justice to the concept of the 'history from below' it is important that prevailing assumptions see a fundamental transformation.

Amithabh Behar and Yamini Aiyar[45] in their article "Networks of Panchayat Women: Civil Society Space for Political Action" analyse the growing success of networks of elected women representatives (EWRs). It clearly demonstrates the significance of micro initiatives in institutionalizing the Panchayati Raj System. While several of these networks were initially set up to equip EWRs with necessary skills and capacities, some have ventured into the political arena. This essay assesses the experience of some of these networks in western and southern India. Given the nature of interventions of networks and associations of EWRs it is also important for the realization of the full potential of these initiatives, to building ties with the feminist movement and attempting to engender governance of Panchayats.

Veena Tucker[46] in her article "Theoretical Perspectives of Women's Empowerment and the Role of NGOs" states the socio-cultural factors determining the status of women and assesses the strategies of empowering women. She also says that empowerment of women is a long term goal which can be supported by non-governmental organisations by setting the step by step approach. Non-governmental organisations (NGOs) need to increase critical awareness about their own functioning by working with other NGOs and forming networks, and coordinating with the government.

Andre Beteille's[47] article on "Empowerment" explains the empowerment process through the expansion of the civil, political and social rights of citizens and says it a laborious and unexciting process. Empowerment through the class struggle was a different story altogether; but that story has now been played out and it offers hardly any new prospect. There is no doubt that prospect of empowerment through caste war; but that is something that will appeal only to those who have put their minds to sleep. So, in the end, the Indian way of securing empowerment for the unempowered seems to be by the safe way of providing, as extensively as possible, quotas on the basis of community, caste and gender. The belief that a perceptible redistribution of power is no more than wishful thinking. He is skeptical about the existing empowerment process and quota system in the Indian scenario.

Gabriele Dietrich[48] in her article "Loss of Socialist Vision and Options before the Women's Movement" explains the evaporation of ideological content at the national, regional and local levels, and addresses not only the economic field, but also other areas of social emancipation. The women's movement too has been co-opted so much into the ideology of 'empowerment' that even the thinking of alternatives has become difficult. Seen in this light, the re-emergence of a 'socialist vision' calls for ideological clarity, self reliance and simple living. Women, 'The Last Colony' have to ally with other internal colonies like *Dalits* and *Adivasis* to make the stall answerable to their needs.

Shilpa Phadke[49] in her article, "Thirty Years on Women's Studies" reflects on the women's movement and states that the women's movement has with varying degrees of success negotiated with the changing socio-political contexts in India. However, change is slow and painful and the lives of a large section of Indian women have only marginally improved. The contemporary Indian women's movement is still accused of being westernized and unIndian. An important task for the movement thus is to vocally locate the feminist struggle in its diverse Indian cultural and historical settings. It is also imperative that the women's movement begins the task of recreating spaces and building bridges so that its various fragments can once again be fitted into the larger jigsaw. In one sense the movement has been overwhelmingly successful in shaping public consciousness and bringing gender issues to national attention.

Smita Mishra Panda[50] in her article "Women's Empowerment through NGO Interventions: A Framework for Assessment" explains about the women's empowerment through NGO interventions and provides a framework for assessment. Also, in this paper an attempt has been made to arrive at an operational definition of empowerment based on literature review. For a proper understanding of the process of empowerment, a systems view is presented in which all the relevant inter-linked elements have been analysed, such as the external agency

(NGO), target group, development project/programme, immediate environments of the target group and external agency, and the macro environment in which the target group and the NGO exist. Further a seven-step process of assessment of women's empowerment is discussed within the systems framework. The steps are—assessments of the macro-environment, the external agency environment, the external agency, the target group environment, the target group, the development programme/project and lastly integration of the assessment process. Such a framework will help the organisations involved in the design, implementation and evaluation of development projects from the point of view of understanding, incorporating and assessing empowerment related issues at the grassroots level.

Vidhu Verma[51] in her article on "Engendering Development: Limits of Feminist Theories and Justice" says recent feminist critiques of development have questioned some fundamental assumptions of feminist political theory; such critiques have also been successful in subverting long-held assumptions of conventional economic development viewed in the context of women's subordination in third world countries. A redefinition of development must not only be about economic growth, but ensure a redistribution of resources, challenge the gender-based division of labour and also seek to provide for an egalitarian basis in social arrangements. Further, as this article argues, any starting point for feminist critiques of development must also seek to link the end of gender oppression to multiple theories of justice—a justice not juridical but one that recognizes the cultural membership of women in the community.

Chris Beasly[52] in her book *What is Feminism? An Introduction to Feminist Theory* explains different types of feminism and explains how they are departing from the traditional fare. The book also says about how to challenge women's subordinate status. Analysis of feminist thought does not simply involve dealing with plurality of types of feminists—a diverse content—but additionally requires consideration of a plurality of standpoints on how to undertake the analysis—that is, consideration of a range of methodological alternatives. This book explains seven types of feminism such as liberal feminism, radical feminism, marxist/socialist feminism, Freudian feminism, Lacanian feminism, French feminism and post-modern feminism.

Amartya Sen[53] in his article "Capability and Well-Being" tries to explore a particular approach to well-being and advantage in terms of a person's ability to do valuable acts or reach a valuable status of being. The expression "capability" was picked to represent the alternative combinations of things a person is able to do or be—the various 'functionings' he or she can achieve. The capability approach is concerned with showing the cogency of a particular space for the evaluation of individual opportunities and successes. In any social calculus in which individual advantages are constitutively important, that space is of potential significance.

In Amartya Sen's[54] *Inequality Re-examined* the claims of equality in social arrangements are analysed. He begins by identifying a common characteristic of virtually all the contemporary ethical approaches to social arrangements. The basic issue that divides the different approaches is not 'whether equality' but 'equality of what?' The practical importance of the latter turns on the pervasive diversity of human beings, which makes equality in one sphere conflict substantially with equality in another. He concentrates on the capability of different persons to achieve valuable functioning. By investigating inequalities related to such categories as class, gender and communities, he demonstrates the far-reaching significance of these conceptual differences, and the force of the proposed approach.

Amartya Sen's[55] work *Development as Freedom* outlines the need for an integrated analysis of economic, social and political activities, involving a variety of institutions and many interactive agencies. It concentrates particularly on the roles and interconnections between certain crucial instrumental freedoms, including economic opportunities, political freedoms, social facilities, transparency guarantees, and protective security. Societal arrangements involving many institutions are investigated in terms of their contribution to enhancing and guaranteeing the substantive freedom of individuals, seen as active agents of change, rather than as passive recipients of dispensed benefits. Expansion of freedom is viewed both as the primary end and as the principal means of development.

Sakiko Fukuda Parr and A.K.Shivakumar[56] have edited a book *Readings in Human Development.* They trace the evolution of the human development approach from its first formulation to the present day. The book provides a lucid illustration of global measures to address human poverty, security and welfare aspects. Health, well-being, and development are the basic tenets of this volume. Articulating development as a widening of choices, an expansion of freedoms and a fulfillment of human rights gives it a distinct edge over the more narrow perception of development as economic expansion alone. Looking ahead, the thinking about poverty and human development will come to be influenced more and more by the agency of human beings—women in particular. Issues of justice, equality and rights will deepen the discourse on human rights and human development.

Ingrid Robeyn's[57] paper on "Sen's Capability Approach and Gender Inequality: Selecting Relevant Capabilities" investigates how Amartya Sen's capability approach can be applied to conceptualizations and assessing gender inequality in western societies. She argues against the endorsement of a definitive list of capabilities and instead defines a procedural approach to the selection of capabilities by proposing five criteria. This procedural account is then used to generate a list of capabilities for conceptualizing gender inequality in western societies. A survey of empirical studies shows that women are worse off than men on some dimensions, better off on a few others, and similarly placed on yet others, while for some dimensions the evaluation is unclear. She outlines why, for group inequalities, inequalities in achieved functionings can be taken to reflect inequalities in capabilities, and how an overall evaluation could be arrived at by weighting the different capabilities.

Amartya Sen[58] in his *Argumentative Indian* explains how gender inequality of one type tends to encourage and sustain gender inequality of other kinds. But, the importance of women's agency and voice reflects itself nearly in every field of social life. Even though for many purposes such simple indicators as women's education, employment and land ownership have much predictive power, there are broader influences on women's agency that also need consideration. It is necessary to widen the focus of attention from women's well-being, seen on its own, to women's agency. He argues that we need a fuller cognizance agency and an adequate appreciation of the fact that women's power and initiative can uplift the lives of all human beings—women, men and children.

Sushama Sahay's[59] *Empowerment of Women: Approaches and Strategies* offers an understanding of the need for empowering women, concept and framework for women's empowerment. Besides, this book also seeks to discuss the various approaches and strategies for empowering women by outlining the mechanisms and tools that women are using for their empowerment. Empowerment in the real sense will be attained when women are actively involved in the larger struggle for social change.

Santosh Gupta's[60] article "Strategy for Empowerment of Women" discusses the empowerment of women as a tool for bringing about organizational competence. Empowerment is a process which has evolved in response to trends towards a greater degree of responsibility and involvement. An attempt has also been made to highlight the potentialities of women executives, which need to be tapped to the benefit of women as well as the organization.

Empirical Review

The empirical review helps in understanding the research gap and field realities.

G. Palanithurai's,[61] "The Genre of Women Leaders in Local Bodies: Experience from Tamil Nadu" explains the process of recruitment of women leaders to the local bodies and how they handle power in their institutions. It analyses the problem of the women leaders while performing their roles and responsibilities. Different types of leaders with varying backgrounds and intentions have come to these positions. In the given environmental setting how they struggle to perform their function has been analysed in this work. It indicates the need of the hour for the women leaders to perform their roles efficiently. At the end of the five years' tenure how the women leaders look at their space and how they design their public life have also been analysed in this article.

G. Palanithurai's,[62] "Impediments of Empowerment of Women: Experiences of Elected Women Representatives in Panchayats in Tamil Nadu" investigates the problems faced by the Elected Women Representatives as they manage the local body institutions. He has classified the nature and intensity of the obstacles and hurdles in the process of governance and explained how these problems are being tackled by them, and with whose support. The article has brought to light the ways and means by which the problem can be tackled, what the need of the leaders is and how they can be met by external agencies.

A.Celine Rani's,[63] *Emerging Pattern of Rural Women Leadership in India* studies the process by which the women leaders are emerging to the political front to manage the Panchayat system. By evolving a framework suitable to this study, the process of emergence of the leaders has been established that the socio-economic status is a significant factor in determining the emergence of rural women leadership. The other factors such as reputation of the family of the leaders will certainly influence the emergence of rural women leaders. Different kinds of categories of leaders have been identified. This reflects the conditions in Tamil Nadu.

Sunita Kishor and Kamla Gupta[64] in their article "Women's Empowerment in India and Its States: Evidence From the NFHS" uses the data from the NFHS-2 to document women's empowerment as a whole and in each of 26 states with 1999 boundaries. In general, it finds that the average woman in India is disempowered absolutely as well as relative to men, and there has been little change in her empowerment over time. This result is obvious no matter how empowerment is measured, be it in terms of the indicators of the evidence, sources or setting for empowerment. However, there is great variation in the level of women's empowerment across the different states and across indicators. The indicators focus on the circumstances of women's lives and reflect the opportunities available to women.

Sudha Pai[65] in her article "Pradhans in New Panchayats: Field Notes from Meerut District" says that the 73rd Constitutional Amendment, which gives women 33 per cent of the seats at all levels of the Panchayat system, has been widely perceived as a crucial step for empowering women. But this brief study of three villages from Meerut District in Uttar Pradesh cautions that unless reservations are accompanied by female literacy, independent voting rights and change in the status in the family and society, women will continue to act as mere namesake representatives of the males of their household. The provision of reservations has not led to women participating in decision-making in local bodies. However, standing for elections and becoming Pradhans has made a difference in the lives of these women.

Maitreyi Das[66] in her article "Mahila Mandals in Gender Politics" explains how Mahila Mandals, traditional local women's organisations, have tremendous potential to address women's strategic gender needs through a study of some Mahila Mandals in Thane, Maharashtra. In rural areas they are increasingly acting as vehicles of resistance that enable women to enter the public domain. In the context of reservation of quotas for women in the rural local elected bodies, the role of Mahila Mandals becomes significant. In order to stand for elections, women need political training, financial and political (not necessarily party) support, networks, and experience. Leadership of Mahila Mandals provides all these prerequisites. On the basis of experience in Thane, it can be argued that Mahila Mandals enable women to enter into the public domain in four ways. First, they allow the majority of their members to engage in action to articulate their practical needs such as water, health, employment, or sanitation. Second, they foster a leadership cadre of privileged women who enter formal politics on the strength of their experience in Mahila Mandals. Third, they serve as the arena for playing out the party politics of the area when they are used by political parties as their women's arms. Fourth, they allow women to question the oppression that is contained in violence and to act against it.

Maitreyi Das's[67] "Women's Autonomy and Politics of Gender in Guyana" explains the condition and position of women in Guyana. This paper is an attempt to analyse the complexities of women's autonomy in Guyana. The Human Development Report 1995 demonstrates that no country in the world treats women as well as it does its men. Even so, the HDR ranks Guyana fairly high on its gender-related indicators. The country ranks high on personal and micro level indicators of women's autonomy; it ranks low on macro and economic indicators. This is mediated by a contradiction between ideology of gender and the living reality. Public policy has given credence to the value of women as domestic actors, even though their lives display active involvement in managing their resources. Thus, women's access to resources has been limited by policies, even though their control of their personal resources is high.

Raghabendra Chattopadhyay and Esther Duflo[68] in their article "Impact of Reservation in Panchayati Raj: Evidence from a Nationwide Randomized Experiment" discuss whether or not reservations make a difference, for political outcomes and governance better reflect the interest of their own groups. A necessary condition for the efficacy of the reservation policy in Panchayat institutions is that elected representatives have independent power and autonomy over and above not only the direct control of the villagers, but also above the control of the bureaucracy, party hierarchies and the local elite. This paper summarises findings from a research project on local decentralization conducted in two districts of West Bengal and Rajasthan. The findings establish that reservation introduced as a tool to ensure adequate representation also assists in adequate delivery of local public goods to disadvantaged groups. Given the evidence that Panchayat leaders make a difference and that bringing women and SCs into politics may help in improving their welfare. Reduced fertility may be achieved by increasing women's bargaining power in the family, and an effective democracy with adequate women's representation may be more effective at achieving it than regulation that takes away from women and SCs what the 73rd Amendment guarantees them.

Srilatha Batliwala, B.K.Anitha, Anitha Gurumurthy and Chandana S.Walli[69] in their book, *Status of Rural Women in Karnataka* analyse the condition and position of rural women in Karnataka. A framework to study women's status has to follow from a clear understanding of gender equality. Studying women's status means a sensitive diagnosis of the nature of gender subordination through the study of gender relation in a specific context. It also means the application of measures derived from a clearly articulated goal of equality to that context. This study explains the impact of major policies and provisions in the areas of law, economic development, health, education, family planning and rural development on women. This was examined by women's access to survival needs, access to food, access to health, profile of asset ownership, occupational status and income categories, control over labour and income, marriage, control over reproduction and sexuality, control over physical mobility, control over physical security, access to education, access to credit, access to other public resources, access to political participation and access to law and justice.

F. Stephen and N. Rajasekaran[70] in their book, *Sheep and Lambs* provide an empirical study of women in local self governance in Karnataka. In their study they identified the achievements of women Gram Panchayat members and constraints at personal, familial and institutional levels. Further they studied the gender role transformation at the household level as a result of political leadership in grassroots democratic institutions. Also, they assessed the impact of training initiatives in strengthening political leadership and empowerment and evolved strategies to counter the constraints in women's political empowerment through legislative and administrative measures. They found that 33.3 per cent reservation has led to the process of political empowerment of women, particularly among the members who have received training and women have realized the importance of education and training for true political empowerment.

Sakuntala Narasimhan's[71] book *Empowering Women: An Alternative Strategy from Rural India* has assessed the effectiveness of an alternative strategy of development and empowerment of women that begins with awareness generation i.e., empowering women psychologically, first with confidence, information and optimism and motivation rather than economic interventions. It also emphasizes the fact that women lag behind men in terms of every set of socio-economic indicators. In spite of gender equality being one of the constitutional mandates, the same kind of imbalances mark the urban-rural divide with a greater percentage of the rural population falling below the poverty line. This study clearly depicts how women fare worse than men in work, employment, earnings, education, health status and decision making powers and that there is a clear difference between male and female entitlements.

Zenab Banu's[72] book *Tribal Women Empowerment and Gender Issues* presents a refreshingly new visit to the issue of empowerment of women. The approach taken in the present study is to analyse the status of tribal women in the light of the 73rd Constitutional Amendment. Basically the problem of social stratification in terms of gender relations has been taken up for the study. When the women have been given power, they control the affairs of the Panchayat Samiti. This puts them higher in the stratification hierarchy. How the difference between males and females has led the tribal to the path of development and how the gender hierarchy of women has been elevated is the focus of the author's enquiry.

G. Palanithurai[73] in his article "Women in Governance for Development at Grassroots" explains how women at the grassroots have perceived the space for governance as development space and most of their governance endeavours address development issues. This article, based on the performance of the Elected Women Representatives of local bodies in Tamil Nadu, shows how in spite of their inexperience these leaders have come to grips with their new assigned role in a partriarchical society. Their perception of this new role has made much of the difference in their approach towards social, developmental and governance related issues. Their transparent working, concern towards the society and ability to lead from front display all the necessary qualities that are attributed to modern concepts of good governance.

G. Palanithurai's[74] "Role of Elected Women Representatives in Evolving Alternative Governance at Grassroots" asserts that it is recognized throughout the world that grassroots women's groups are redefining governance and development in their orbit of action. They significantly alter the process of administering development. By their local action significant progress and changes are made in the life of the communities, which in turn, draw the attention of the academics, administrators and the media. The experiences of fifty-two Gram Panchayats headed by women in Tamil Nadu, proved that the elected women representatives consider the space, which they occupy as a space for development. They tend to seek a support base for their activities, especially for increasing their efficiency and capability. They develop alternative governance to achieve development with the participation of the people.

Sandra Grey[75] in her paper "Women and Parliamentary Politics: Does Size Matter? Critical Mass and Women MPs in the New Zealand House of Representatives" outlines the expectations in existing critical mass literature and tests these using the New Zealand House of Representatives as a case study. It is often claimed that women will only impact women political decisions once they achieve a critical mass within legislation bodies. What the New Zealand case highlighted was the number of complexities that are ignored in critical mass literature and the likelihood that different critical masses are necessary dependent on the outcome sought.

Donley T.Studlar[76] and Ian McAllister in their paper "Does a Critical Mass Exist? A Comparative Analysis of Women's Legislative Representation, 1949-1997" examine one of the less-explored dimensions of the critical mass concept: is there a process by which women reaching a critical mass of the legislature accelerate the election of further women? Using data from the Inter-Parliamentary Union and International Institute of Democracy and Electoral Assistance, they analyze this question for 17 industrialized democracies over a period of almost half a century. Descriptive results indicate that gains in women's representation have been incremental rather than a critical mass accelerating the election of women to legislatures. In a multivariate analysis of the percentage of women in the lower house of the legislature, the critical mass is tested against established explanations of women's gains in seats: institutional rules, egalitarian, political culture, political parties, women's educational achievements, and economic development of two measures of the critical mass theory, one has no impact, and the second results in only a small increase in women's gains. Far from being clearly demonstrated, critical mass theories need empirical testing.

Pippa Norris and Joni Lovenduski[77] in their study "Blair's Babes: Critical Mass Theory, Gender and Legislative Life" suggests that once the party takes control, there are no significant differences among women and men leaders. The evidence consistently suggests that women leaders in all the major British parties do bring a different set of values to issues affecting women's equality in the workplace, home, and public sphere. If these attitudes are translated into party manifestos, political debate and ultimately legislative action, for example by shaping policies towards equal pay, reproductive rights, and the adoption of affirmative action strategies in the recruitment of women within parties, then the entry of more women leaders into Westminster has the capacity to make more than simply a symbolic difference.

Kathleen A. Bratton[78] in her paper "Critical Mass Theory Revisited: The Behaviour and Success of Token Individuals in State Legislatives" argue that women in 'skewed' legislatures—that is, legislatures in which women make up less than 15 per cent of the membership—may actually be encouraged to develop legislative agendas that are distinct from those of their male colleagues, and that they may be as successful as their male counterparts. Analysing data from three state legislatures in four years, the author found that even in extremely skewed state legislatures, women are often more active than men in sponsoring legislation that focuses on women's interests; indeed, in two states, gender differences narrow as the legislature becomes more gender diverse. So she concludes that a 'critical mass' is not necessary for substantive representation on the part of individual female state legislators, but that increased diversity may indeed bring about changes in policy outputs.

Evelin Hust[79] in the book *Women's Political Representation and Empowerment in India — A Million Indiras Now?* has attempted to examine the process of women's political presence following the reservation for women in the Panchayati Raj Institutions and its linkage and translation into empowerment, taking two blocks—Gania and Balipatna in Orissa—for detailed empirical study. Two important areas, namely, the symbolic recognition of women's political role and the new access that women have now gained to their elected representatives, were singled out as important changes for the better. On the other hand, the limited room for policy formulations in the institutions of local governance meant that village women have not gained much in material terms and there are hardly any effects that could be attributed to changed policy priorities resulting from women's inclusion in politics. This study effectively establishes that the reservation for women is a step towards women's empowerment.

But it questions the size of this step as well as the social context in which this step is taken.

Isabelle Allane and Jacques Veron's[80] edited book *Gender Discriminations among Young Children in Asia* is a compilation of papers presented at a seminar. Female deficit or the 'missing girls' phenomenon in five Asian countries (India, Pakistan, China, Korea and Taiwan) is featured in this book. All of them highlight the strong preference for son. The four papers on India highlight the situation in some of the worst affected states with sex ratio figures over a period of time. In all the papers changing trends are well documented and the analyses raise various queries. They show that neither higher educational levels nor mere economic development by itself can bring about a change in the mindset towards the girl child and that the outlook and attitude of society towards women need to be transformed and the mental block removed.

Pitam Singh and J.K. Pundir's[81] "Study on Women Legislators in Uttar Pradesh" attempts to analyse the background, role and involvement of women in politics in Uttar Pradesh from the first election in 1952 to 1996. A majority of the women legislators, the study reveals, have a political family background, are educated and economically well-to-do. However, due to their low numerical strength, the women legislators' participation in discussions and assembly proceedings has been low.

Jean Drage's[82] "Women in Local Government in Asia and the Pacific: A Comparative Report" draws together a picture of women's involvement in local government in Asia and the Pacific region. It is based on 13 country reports highlighting continuing barriers to women's involvement in local government, initiatives that have increased women's participation and the transformative leadership that women provide in local government. It also outlines regional and country-level strategies for increasing women's involvement in local government.

Ishrat Shamin and Ranjana Kumari's[83] "Study on Gender and Local Governance: A New Discourse in Development" attempts to analyse the emerging scenario of women leadership in local politics by focusing on the elected women representatives of union parishads of Bangladesh compared to their counterparts in Panchayats of India. It was evident that lack of effective and timely planning, lack of political background, absence of proper socio-economic and political environment, lack of appropriate organizational framework, lack of skill and training placed women behind to prove their competencies compared to their men counterparts.

Sharma and Manisha Gupta[84] in their article say that despite the enactment of laws, formulation of reformative legal processes, provision of legal aid to the needy, extensive use of the provision of public interest litigation, conduct of family courts, women/family counseling centres etc., women in India have a long way to go in concretizing their constitutional goals into reality. Low rates of participation, lack of economic independence, value biases operating against them, etc. have resulted in women being dependent on men folk and other institutions of authority like the family, the neighborhood and the society. They are usually ignorant of their rights and even if they are not, they do not have easy access to justice.

The Asian Development Bank[85] in its report on "Gender and Governance Issues in Local Government" focused on gender and local governance in Bangladesh, Nepal and Pakistan. This report was based on a project which focused on the efforts to apply the three pillars of the Asian Development Bank's poverty reduction strategy at the grassroots level. The project designed a framework for promoting gender and good governance to assist women representatives to carry out their roles more confidently and to serve their constituents, who are mainly poor women, more effectively.

Sarala Gopalan's[86] *Situational Analysis of Women and Girls in Tamil Nadu* presents a unique situation of the status of women and girl children in Tamil Nadu. The state has not been able to consistently translate its record of economic growth into sustained improvements in the quality of people's lives. There seems to be a widening of the gap between growth and human development. It is necessary for the state to re-establish the linkages between growth and improvements in human development. Conversion of incomes into human development is mediated, among other things, by the levels of public spending on social development by efficiency improvements in the public provisioning of basic social services, and by better planning and policy formulation.

Research Gap Identified from the Review

The review of literature identifies the following research gap:

1. Most of the studies discuss the problems faced by women in general.

2. Considerable number of studies state women's empowerment can be attained through state's benevolence.
3. Studies do not refer to the issues of gender and women in the process of governance.
4. It is rare to find a study which identifies the freedom enjoyed and opportunity available for elected women representatives.
5. There is hardly a study dealing with the ability of women leaders to bring about substantial change in the process of governance favouring women folk.

To sum up, there is no comprehensive study available which deals with the freedom enjoyed by elected women representatives and the functioning manifested by them on gender issues. At this moment it is essential to know how elected women representatives in grassroots governance influence the process of governing gender issues. It is important to examine the level of freedom enjoyed by EWRs in the socio-economic political sphere and evaluate the functioning manifested by the EWRs on gender issues.

Issues Raised from the Review

1. To what extent women in grassroots governance affect governance amidst the resistance from sexual hierarchical society?
2. What are the tangible indicators available to measure the freedom enjoyed by EWRs and the functioning manifested by them on gender issues?

It is with these assumptions that a study has been proposed to examine the capability of elected women representatives on gender issues in grassroots governance.

Theoretical Framework

Almost in all states, at least two rounds of elections for local bodies have been held after the states amended their laws to bring them in conformity with the 73rd and 74th Constitutional Amendment Acts of India. Reservation of seats for women in local governance is a positive step for women and it has become necessary to asses the extent to which this action has affected women's position in Indian society. The critical mass of women in political life should increase their capability. The theory of critical mass suggests that there will be a qualitative change in the nature of group interaction, as the minority starts asserting itself and thereby transforming institutional culture, norms and values.[87] This theory can also be applied to the position of women in decision-making. As more women occupy the political space, the culture will change, the agenda of politics will broaden, and the institution will be transformed.

In political science women's representation and participation in decision-making bodies are looked at against the backdrop of the 'critical mass' which refers to the quantity needed to start a chain reaction, an irreversible takeoff into a new situation of process.[88] Based on the studies conducted, Drude Dahlerup lists the changes to be expected when women achieve the critical mass. They include change of political discourse, social climate of political life, policies, culture, behaviour, political attitudes, policy priorities, legislative styles and decision-making roles.[89] Therefore it becomes necessary to examine the postulates evolved over a period of time on the basis of the experience in the wide world of women's way of governing.[90]

Of the several assumptions about women in governance in the world, for this study a few are considered vital and relevant to the Indian context. G. Palanithurai has worked extensively in this context. According to him, first, women will bring a different approach to governance. It is a strong notion among development organizations and women activist groups who have rich experience with women that women will bring in new ideas, nuances, energy, enthusiasm and approach to governance and that hitherto unutilized potentials will be used. It is expected that women's participation will transform the quality of the political life and agenda.[91]

Second, Elected Women Representatives play an important role in pushing women's issues forward for public discussion and decision making. It is pertinent to mention here the view that women have been oriented to think like men as patriarchy is strongly entrenched in the family and the social system. They do have their own distinctive thought process. But there is no space for it in the public fora. On certain issues, Elected Women Representatives show greater concern in the decision making process. It is true that they are not in one group. They have their own different affiliations. In order to bring the women's issues to the public they need a support structure. They establish links with-Self Help Groups (SHGs) and through them the issues of women are being discussed. They are also divided on caste, class and religion. Yet they show their distinctiveness in the process of governance.[92]

Third, Elected Women Representatives ensure more participation of the people in the process of development and governance. Women leaders at the grassroots in the Indian context always evince simplicity, transparency and accountability. They further demonstrate that they maintain their closeness and contact with the clients and the people.[93]

Fourth, Elected Women Representatives have different sets of skills and they enhance the leadership qualities of others. Women have developed skills to carry out works despite the limited resources and differences of opinion with their family members. Working in adverse circumstances is not new to them. Further they have patience to listen to others, which men do not have. On many occasions Elected Women Representatives are honest and accurate in presenting issues to the decision-making authorities.[94]

Fifth, Elected Women Representatives are the pathfinders in attacking social issues. They assume powers to perform certain roles and responsibilities. Several of the problems which need to be attended to required no power. Women leaders who have a service orientation in their attitudes and behaviour, assume responsibilities and carry out activities in society and they become role models and they are able to set new agendas and perhaps create new styles of leadership.[95]

With these few propositions, the present study analyses the role of Elected Women Representatives on gender issues in grassroots governance. Dahlerup argues that by attaining a critical mass of women, rather than a token few, the political norms and the political culture can be changed. Of several assumptions about women in governance and their impact on the society, Palanithurai's propositions can form the theoretical base of the present study which are considered vital and relevant to the Indian context.

Analytical Framework

The focus on the role of women in governance has a direct bearing on women's well-being which has its reach beyond that. Nothing, arguably, is as important today in the political economy of development as an adequate recognition of political, economic and social participation and leadership of women.[96] The intervention of women in the process of governance aroused the interest to study the impact created by women in grassroots governance with particular reference to their performance in solving gender issues for the welfare of women. This functioning of EWRs can be termed as the 'agency' which refers to the pursuit of goals and objectives that a person has reason to value and advance, whether or not they are connected with the person's own well-being.[97]

The first reason for the importance of women's agency is, thus, the persistence of gender-based inequalities of well-being, given the relevance of women's actions and movements in bringing about a change in this field.[98] People may actively choose to pursue other objectives (that is, other than personal well-being), which could, quite possibly, be very broad, such as independence of one's country, the elimination of famines and epidemics, or (related to the present context) the removal of gender inequality in general. Perhaps the most immediate argument for focusing on women's agency is precisely the role that agency can play in removing the inequities that depress the well-being of women. Women are, in this broadened perspective, not passive recipients of welfare enhancing help brought about by society, but are active promoters and facilitators of social transformation. Such transformations influence, of course, the lives and well being of women, but also those of men and all children, boys as well as girls.[99] This will help to analyse the outcome of the empowerment process created through the reservation of seats in the local bodies' decision making position. Hence, this study analyses the role of EWRs on gender issues in grassroots governance.

The present study can be divided into two parts. The first part traces the instrumental factors which help in the formation of capabilities of EWRs to perform their roles and responsibilities in the sphere of governance for the welfare of women. These instrumental factors largely depend upon the social and power structure. The instrumental factors can be called the "principal means" which concern the different kinds of rights, opportunities and entitlements for women in governance to exercise their roles and responsibilities. These tend to contribute to the general capability of EWRs and expansion of their freedom to solve gender issues.

In the second part, the acquired capabilities of EWRs will be evaluated by analysing their performance in solving gender issues which ultimately helps to enhance the status of women in rural India. The acquired capabilities and their performance can be evaluated by their way of functioning. Functioning represents the various things that women manages to do in solving gender issues. The capability of EWRs reflects the alternative combinations of functioning they can achieve and from which they can choose one collection. These alternative combinations of functioning will be the various strategies adopted by the EWRs to solve the issues of gender in their respective areas. These strategies can be derived from the Conformity Act to the 73rd Constitutional Amendment Act as well as from the adoption of their own choices. Their chosen strategy may lead to the achievement of solving gender issues and enriching the life of rural women folk. This can be termed as the 'primary end' where EWRs can bring about substantive change in the lives of women.

Therefore this study analyses the "principal means" and the "primary ends" of women in governance in working for the welfare of women. Nobel Laureate Amartya Sen calls these two roles the expansion of freedom in his "capability approach". The present study will adopt the capability approach propounded by Amartya Sen.

Capability approach is a broad normative framework which evaluates the social arrangements and the extent of freedom people have to promote or achieve functionings they value. It examines what people are actually able to do, the range of alternatives they face while doing the function they value and to what extent they make decisions that matter to them. Capability is primarily a reflection of the freedom to achieve valuable functionings. It concentrates directly on freedom as such rather than on the means to achieve freedom, and it identifies the real alternatives they have.[100] The object is to concentrate on the individual's real opportunity to pursue her objectives.

A person's "capability" refers to the alternative combinations of functionings that are feasible for her to achieve. Capability is thus a kind of freedom, the substantive freedom to achieve alternative functioning combinations (or, less formally put, the freedom to achieve various lifestyles). The extent of each functioning possible to a person may be represented by a real number, and when this is done, a person's actual achievement can be seen as a functioning vector. The "capability set" would then consist of the alternative functioning vectors that she can choose from. While the combination of a person's functioning's reflects her actual achievements, the capability set represents the freedom to achieve the alternative functioning combinations form which this person can choose.

According to Amartya Sen, the evaluative focus of this capability approach is on what a person is actually able to do and the real opportunities available to her to perform the function she has reason to value. The performance of her function is influenced directly or indirectly by certain instrumental factors. These factors Sen calls the principal means or the instrumental roles of freedom which influences the overall freedom people have to live the way they would like to live. Sen classifies the instrumental freedom broadly into five:

1. Political freedoms,
2. Economic facilities,
3. Social opportunities,
4. Transparency guarantees, and
5. Protective security.

These instrumental freedoms tend to contribute to the general capability of a person to live more freely, but also serve to complement one another. These freedoms give the appropriate space and the capabilities to choose a life one has reason to value. With these principal means, the primary end can be achieved, called by Sen the constitutive role of freedom, which relates to the importance of substantive freedom in enriching human life. The capability approach directs one to look at conditions that influence women's internal development and also at conditions of the material and social environment that influence their ability to turn their ideas into action.

By adopting the normative proposition of Amartya Sen's capability approach, the present study analyses the capability of EWRs in solving gender issues. All formulations of capability have two parts: freedom and functionings. Freedom helps to empower EWRs themselves for their own development and for the development of the community. Functioning represents the various things EWRs may value doing for solving gender issues.

In order to perform the functions which improve the lives of women, the freedom enjoyed by EWRs should be analysed, which Sen calls the "Primary means". The extent of freedom they enjoy in the political space, availability of economic facilities, social opportunities and the provision of transparency guarantees and protective security will be taken into account. This freedom ultimately results in their range of functioning's. There may be many functioning elements available to EWRs to solve gender issues. This may be known or may not be known to the EWRs and it depends upon the freedom they enjoy. The alternative functioning element available to the EWRs to solve the issues of gender are known as "capability set" and this will be identified in the study. The achievement of EWRs by utilizing the combination of various functioning elements from the "capability set" is known as "functioning vector". Through this "functioning vector" the performance of EWRs will be analysed in enhancing the life of women in rural areas which Sen calls the "primary end".

Objectives of the Study

The study has the following objectives:

1. To examine the level of freedom enjoyed by EWRs in the socio-economic political sphere.
2. To evaluate the functioning manifested by the EWRs on gender issues.
3. To explore the relationship between the freedom enjoyed by EWRs and the functioning they manifested on the gender issues.

Hypothesis

The greater the freedom enjoyed by the EWRs the greater the functioning manifested by them.

Methodology

Study Design

This study relies mainly on primary data. The data were collected from women village Panchayat presidents. Among the three tiers, the village Panchayat occupies a prominent position where rural people have direct access to the process of governance and concepts like participation, transparency and accountability become operationalised. Therefore Elected Women Representatives, at the village Panchayat president level have been chosen for the study.

For the selection of respondents it was proposed to make a census survey of women village Panchayat Presidents in Dindigul District.

The census survey method was adopted in order to cover all the study units. Dindigul District was chosen for the study because gender development in the district is lower than the Human Development Index. Moreover this is a backward district and the influence of caste is predominant. There are 306 village Panchayats in Dindigul District and 106 village Panchayats are reserved for women. Totally 112 village Panchayats are headed by women. It is interesting to note that six women contested and came out successful in constituencies not reserved for women. Out of 112 village Panchayats only 109 respondents turned up for the study since the researcher could not meet three women due to various reasons. Out of these three women Panchayat Presidents, one woman got married and went to her husband's house which is outside the district. Her father takes care of the Panchayat activities and she remains the titular head. Another woman lost her husband and became a widow and she was reluctant to meet outsiders. The third woman, who is very old did not want to answer the questions and said that she did not know anything. Therefore only 109 elected women representatives were interviewed out of the 112 elected women representatives in Dindigul district.

Measuring Indicators

Freedom and the functioning of EWRs will be examined and evaluated by adopting the following indicators:

Freedom (Independent Variable)

Variables			*Indicators*
1. Political Freedom	–	(i)	Access to and control over political space
		(ii)	Access to and control over government schemes
		(iii)	Position held in other organisations
		(iv)	Support from Ward Members/ Block/District Panchayat
2. Economic Facilities	–	(i)	Occupation & Family annual income
		(ii)	Her previous occupation

Variables		*Indicators*
	(iii)	Access & control over assets
	(iv)	Management of budget at home
	(v)	Ability to create profitable assets in Panchayat
3. Social Opportunities –	(i)	Education
	(ii)	Physical mobility
	(iii)	Training
	(iv)	Confidence to speak in public
	(v)	Awareness on issues affecting women
	(vi)	Negotiating power within family/community
	(vii)	Existence of a vision of the future
	(viii)	Extent to which other household members help her
	(ix)	Respect from community
4. Transparency Guarantees –	(i)	Access to information
	(ii)	Entitlement to seek redressal
	(iii)	Lack of corruption
5. Protective Security –	(i)	Legal remedies
	(ii)	Official/community/family support
	(iii)	Affiliation with NGO/CBO/ EWR Federation

Functioning (Dependent Variable)

Variables		*Indicators*
1. Creating Awareness on Gender Issues –	(i)	Informing and educating the public about the ill-effects of gender discrimination and related issues through folk arts/pamphlets/notices/rally/ hoardings
	(ii)	Gender sensitization programme

Variables		Indicators
		(iii) Informing women about their rights
2. Administrative Action	–	(i) Resolution passed in Gram Sabha to solve gender issues
		(ii) Committee for women
		(iii) Plan for women and girl children development
		(iv) Involving people in activities for the welfare of women
		(v) Budget allocation for women and girl children
3. Services provided to women	–	(i) Water
		(ii) Health care
		(iii) Sanitation
		(iv) Action against (illicit) liquor
		(v) Action against atrocities on women
4. Ensuring women's participation in social and political activities	–	(i) Making women attend Gram Sabha
		(ii) Making women participate in the activities of the Panchayat
		(iii) Seeking women's help at the time of any issues affecting women
5. Organising struggle on issues affecting women	–	(i) Bringing women together on issues affecting women
		(ii) Deciding on common action
		(iii) Forging common ideologies
6. Women development activities	–	(i) Approaching sectoral department for women welfare programmes
		(ii) Vocational training for women
		(iii) Assistance to destitute and deserted women
		(iv) Formation and assistance to SHG women

Variables		*Indicators*
		(v) Assistance to SC/ST women
		(vi) Assistance for marriage/ education/maternity benefits
		(vii) Employment opportunity for women
		(viii) Ensuring equal wages for women
		(ix) Eliminating gender disparity in school education
7. Creating support structure	–	(i) Building alliance with NGO/ SHG/women organisations
		(ii) Member of Elected Women Representatives Federation
8. Problem solving mechanism	–	(i) Legal remedies
		(ii) Negotiation

Tools for Data Collection

Data were collected from the elected women village Panchayat presidents of Dindigul district. An interview schedule was prepared to collect data from the respondents. Informal discussions were also held to prepare case studies.

Sources of Data

The data required for this study were drawn from both secondary and primary sources. Secondary data were obtained from government publications, census report, academic publications, reports etc. Primary data were collected from the elected women village Panchayat presidents.

Scoring and Analysis

The answers to the schedule were scored on a two point scale as hereunder.

Yes = One (1)
No = Zero (0)

Equal weight was given to each question. It is, therefore, easy and ideal to compare between one and another. Correlation and regression method was used to explore the relationship between freedom (Independent Variable) and functioning (Dependent Variable) of EWRs on gender issues. Moreover, it would be ideal to assign some weight for each indicator to derive a score as economists or psychologists do. But this can be done when indicators are in the right order. Since this study dealt with the Panchayat, a grassroots institution, it was difficult to arrange the indicators in the right order and assign weights following this order. Again, there was a problem of priorities. This was because different respondents were found to have different priorities based on their economic and social conditions. It was therefore decided to use a two point scale to derive an individual score rather than compute some weight.

Stages of the Study

In order to collect the required data from the sample selected for the study, field work was conducted in Dindigul district, Tamil Nadu. The field work was carried out in two stages: pilot study and the main study.

Pilot Study

A pilot study was considered necessary to understand the nature of the sample and to verify the appropriateness of the tools and to get an initial feedback on the problem set for the study. Based on the pilot study necessary changes were made and the tools were finalized.

Main Study

The main field work was carried out during the year 2006.

Operational Definition

1. **Capability:** Capability denotes attainable options available to individuals. For this study it is defined as what women village Panchayat presidents are actually able to do, the range of alternatives they face while doing the functions they value and the extent to which they make decisions matter to them.
2. **Freedom:** Freedom represents the various opportunities available for the women village Panchayat presidents to equip themselves to tackle gender issues.

3. **Functioning:** Functioning represents the functions manifested by the women village Panchayat presidents to tackle gender issues.
4. **Gender Issues:** Gender issues may be defined as the problems faced by women because of their relative deprivation by men due to the influence of a patriarchal, stratified society.

Chapterization

The study is presented in seven chapters. The first chapter introduces the study and presents the problem and its rationale, the review of literature, the analytical framework, states the objectives of the study and the methodology. The second chapter presents the status of women and an overview of decentralized governance with special reference to Tamil Nadu. The third chapter deals with the freedom enjoyed by EWRs in the socio-economic-political sphere. The fourth chapter deals with the functioning of EWRs on gender issues. The fifth chapter deals with the relationship between the freedom enjoyed by EWRs and the functioning they manifested on gender issues. The sixth chapter presents the integrated analysis. The seventh chapter presents the summary and the policy prescriptions.

REFERENCES

1. Jean Dreze and Amartya Sen, *India: Development and Participation,* New Delhi: Oxford University Press, 2002.
2. Amartya Sen, *Development as Freedom,* New Delhi: Oxford University Press, 2005.
3. UNDP, *Human Development Report 2006*, Oxford: Oxford University Press, 2006.
4. Mahabubul Haq Human Development Centre, *Human Development in South Asia: The Gender Question,* Oxford University Press, 2000.
5. Ishrat Shamin and Ranjana Kumari, "Gender and Local Governance: A New Discourse in Development", Report Submitted to South Asia Network of Economic Research Institutes, Submitted by Centre for Women and Children Studies, Dhaka, Bangladesh and Centre for Social Research, New Delhi: India, November 2002.
6. Drude Dahlerup, "Using quotas to increase women's political representation", in Karam, Azza (ed), *Women in Parliament: Beyond*

Numbers, Stockholm: The International Institute for Democracy and Electoral Assistance, 1998

7. G. Palanithurai, *Grassroots Democracy in Indian Society,* New Delhi: Concept Publishing Company, 2000.
8. D.Bandopadhyay, "Gender and Governance in India", *Economic and Political Weekly,* July 29, 2000.
9. Wandana Sonalkar, "An Agenda of Gender Politics", *Economic and Political Weekly,* January 9, 1999.
10. Farida Vahedi, "Gender Equality and Social Responsibility", *Sarvodaya,* Sep-Oct, 2003.
11. Shobhita Rajagopal and Kanchan Mathur, "Women's Empowerment through State Benevolence", *Economic and Political Weekly*, August 12, 2000.
12. B. Suguna, "Women's Empowerment: Concept and Framework", *Social Welfare*, December 2001.
13. Vina Mazumdar, "Women: From Equality and Empowerment" in Hiranmay Karlekar (ed), *Independent India: The First Fifty Years,* New Delhi: Oxford University Press, 1998.
14. Indhrani Sridharan, "Practising Human Rights: A Feminist Perspective" in Chiranjivi J.Nirmal (ed), *Human Rights in India: Historical, Social and Political Perspectives,* New Delhi: Oxford University Press, 2000.
15. Shobna Sonpar and Ravi Kapur, "Non-Conventional Indicators: Gender Disparities under Structural Reforms", *Economic and Political Weekly,* Jan 6, 2001.
16. Nirmala Buch, *Women's Experience in New Panchayats: The Emerging Leadership of Rural Women,* Occasional Paper No:35, New Delhi: Centre for Women's Development Studies, 2000.
17. Jennie Litvack, Junaid Ahmad, Richard Bird, *Rethinking Decentralization in Developing countries,* Washington D.C.: The World Bank, 1998.
18. Kamla Bhasin, *Understanding Gender,* New Delhi: Kali for Women, 2000
19. B.K. Nagla, "Sex and Gender: Cognitive Analysis" in Abha Avasthi, A.K. Srivastava (eds), *Modernity, Feminism and Women Empowerment,* New Delhi: Rawat Publications, 2001.
20. Naila Kabeer, *Reversed Realities: Gender Hierarchies in Development Thought,* New Delhi: Kali for Women, 1994.
21. Asha Ramesh and Bharti Ali, *33 1/3 per cent Reservation towards Political Empowerment,* Bangalore: Books for Change, 2001.
22. Martha C.Nussbaum, *Human Capabilities: Women, Culture and Development,* New York: Oxford University Press, 1996.
23. Jean Dreze and Amartya Sen, *India: Development and Participation,* New Delhi: Oxford University Press, 2002.
24. Anupama Roy, "Community, Women Citizens and a Women's Politics", *Economic and Political Weekly,* April 28, 2001.
25. Karunakar Patnaik, "Devolution of Powers to Panchayati Raj Institutions in India: An Overview", *The Grassroots Governance Journal,* Vol.1, No.2, Dec 2003.

26. Rehana Ghadially (ed), *Women in Indian Society,* New Delhi: Sage Publications, 1988.
27. A.M.Shah, B.S. Baviskar, E.A. Ramaswamy (Eds), *Social Structure and Change: Women in Indian Society,* Vol.2, New Delhi: Sage Publications, 1992.
28. J.P. Singh, "Indian Democracy and Empowerment of Women", *The Indian Journal of Public Administration,* Vol.XLVI, No.4, Oct-Dec, 2000.
29. Carol le Bacchi, *The Politics of Affirmative Action: Women, Equality and Category Politics,* London: Sage Publications, 2003.
30. Maitrayee Mukhopadhyay, "Creating Citizens Who Demand Just Governance: Gender and Development in the twenty first century" Gender and Development Vol.11, No.3, Nov, 2003.
31. UNDP, *Essays on Gender and Governance,* New Delhi: Human Development Resource Centre and United National Development Programme, 2003.
32. Human Development Resource Centre, *Decentralization in India: Challenges and Opportunities:* Discussion Paper Series-1, New Delhi: UNDP, 2001.
33. UNDP, *Women's Political Participation and Good Governance: 21st Century Challenges,* New Delhi: HDRC, UNDP, 2000.
34. Kamla Bhasin, *What is Patriarchy,* New Delhi: Kali for Women, 2000.
35. Kamla Bhasin and Nighat Said Khan, *Some Questions on Feminism and its Relevance in South Asia,* New Delhi: Kali for Women, 2000.
36. Urban Governance Toolkit Series, *Local to Local Dialogue: A Grassroots Women's Perspective on Good Governance,* Nairobi: UN-HABITAT and Huairou Commission, Sep 2004.
37. Emma Bell, *Emerging Issues in Gender and Development: An Overview,* Sussex: Institute of Development Studies, University of Sussex, November 2000.
38. Stephanie Tawa Lama-Rewal, "Fluctuating, Ambivalent Legitimacy of Gender as a Political Category", *Economic and Political Weekly,* Apr 28, 2001.
39. Esther Duflo, *Why Political Reservations?* MIT: Department of Economics and Poverty Action Lab, Sep 2004.
40. James Manor, *The Political Economy of Democratic Decentralization,* Washington D.C.: The World Bank, March 1999.
41. Bidyut Mohanty and Shashi Narayana (eds), *Women and Political Empowerment,* Bangalore: Institute of Social Sciences, 2001.
42. Kumud Sharma, "Institutionalizing Feminist Agenda(s)", *Economic and Political Weekly,* Oct 25, 2003.
43. Maithreyi Krishnaraj, "Challenges before women's Movement in a changing context", *Economic and Political Weekly,* Oct 25, 2003.
44. Vinay Bahl, "What Went Wrong With 'History from Below'", *Economic and Political Weekly,* Jan 11, 2003.

45. Amitabh Behar, Yamini Aiyar, "Networks of Panchayat Women: Civil Society Space for Political Action" *Economic and Political Weekly,* Nov 22, 2003.
46. Veena Tucker, "Theoretical Perspectives of Women's Empowerment and the Role of NGOs", *Women's Link,* Vol.9, No.3, July-Sep, 2003.
47. Andre Beteille, "Empowerment", *Economic and Political Weekly,* March 6-13, 1999.
48. Gabriele Dietrich, "Loss of Socialist Vision and Options before the Women's movement", *Economic and Political Weekly,* Oct 25, 2003.
49. Shilpa Phadke, "Thirty years on Women's Studies Reflects on the Women's Movement", *Economic and Political Weekly,* Oct 25, 2003.
50. Smita Mishra Panda, "Women's Empowerment through NGO Interventions: A Framework for Assessment", *Social Change,* Vol.30, Nos.3&4, Sep-Dec, 2000.
51. Vidhu Verma, "Engendering Development: Limits of Feminist Theories and Justice", *Economic and Political Weekly,* Dec 4, 2004.
52. Chris Beasley, *What is Feminism? An Introduction to Feminist Theory,* London: Sage Publications, 1999.
53. Amartya Sen, "Capability and Well Being" in Martha Nussbaum and Amartya Sen (Eds), *The Quality of life,* New Delhi: Oxford University Press, 2000.
54. Amartya Sen, *Inequality re-examined,* New Delhi: Oxford University Press, 2002.
55. Amartya Sen, *Development As Freedom,* New Delhi: Oxford University Press, 2005.
56. Sakiko Fukuda —Parr and A.K.Shivakumar (Eds), *Readings in Human Development: Concepts, Measures and Policies for a Development Paradigm,* New Delhi: Oxford University Press, 2004.
57. Ingrid Robeyn, "Sen's Capability Approach and Gender Inequality: Selecting Relevant Capabilities", *Feminist Economics* (2), 2003.
58. Amartya Sen, *The Argumentative India: Writings on Indian History, Culture and identity,* London: Allen Lane an Imprint of Penguin Books, 2005.
59. Sushama Sahay, *Women and Empowerment,* New Delhi: Discovery Publishing House, 1998.
60. Santosh Gupta, "Strategy for Empowerment of Women", *Indian Journal of Marketing,* Vol.XXXIII, No.6, June 2003.
61. G. Palanithurai, "The Genre of Women Leaders in Local Bodies: Experience from Tamil Nadu", *The Indian Journal of Public Administration,* Vol.XLVII, No.1, Jan-Mar 2001.
62. G. Palanithurai, "Impediments to Empowerment of Women: Experience of Elected Women Representatives in Panchayats in Tamil Nadu", *The Indian Journal of Political Science,* Vol.63, No.1, March 2002.
63. Celine Rani, *Emerging Pattern of Rural Women Leadership in India,* New Delhi: Kalpaz Publications, 2002.

64. Sunita Kishor and Kamla Gupta, "Women's Empowerment in India and its States: Evidence from NFHS", *Economic and Political Weekly*, Oct 25, 2003.
65. Sudha Pai, "Pradhanis in New Panchayats: Field Notes from Meerut District", *Economic and Political Weekly,* May 2, 1999.
66. Maitreyi Das, "Mahila Mandals in Gender Politics", *Economic and Political Weekly,* Dec 9, 2000.
67. Maitreyi Das, "Women's Autonomy and Politics of Gender in Guyana", *Economic and Political Weekly*, June 3, 2000.
68. Ragabendra Chattopadhyay and Esther Duflo, "Impact of Reservation in Panchayati Raj: Evidence from a Nationwide Randomized Experiment", *Economic and Political Weekly,* Feb 28, 2004.
69. Srilatha Batliwala, B.K. Anitha, Anita Gurumurthy, Chandan S.Wali, *Status of Rural Women in Karnataka,* Bangalore: National Institute of Advanced Studies, 1998.
70. F.Stephen and N.Rajasekaran, *Sheep and Lambs: An Empirical Study of Women in Local Self Governance in Karnataka,* Bangalore: A Search Publication, 2001.
71. Sakuntala Narasimhan, *Empowering Women: An Alternative Strategy from Rural India,* New Delhi: Sage Publications, 1999.
72. Zenab Banu, *Tribal Women Empowerment and Gender Issues,* New Delhi: Kanishka Publishers & Distributors, 2001.
73. G. Palanithurai, "Women in Governance for Development at Grassroots", *The Indian Journal of Public Administration,* Vol.1, No.1, Jan-Mar, 2004.
74. G. Palanithurai, "Role of Elected Women Representatives in Evolving Alternative Governance at Grassroots", *Social Change and Development,* Vol.3, July 2005.
75. Sandra Grey, "Women and Parliamentary Politics: Does Size Matter? Critical Mass and Women MPs in the Newzeland House of Representatives", paper for the 51st Political Studies Association Conferences 10-12 April 2001, Manchester, United Kingdom.
76. Donely T.Studlar and Ian McAllister, "Does a Critical Mass Exist? A Comparative Analysis of Women's Legislative Representation — 1949-1997", paper presented at the American Political Science Association, Atlanta, GA, Sept 2-5, 1999.
77. Pippa Norris and Joni Lovenduski, "Blair's Babes: Critical Mass Theory, Gender and Legislative Life" paper for the women and public policy weekly seminar, 1.00-2.30, Friday 28th Sep 2001, Fainsod Room, Kennedy School of Government.
78. Kathleen A. Bratton, "Critical Mass Theory Revisited: The Behaviour and Success of Token Individuals in State Legislatures", paper presented at the annual meeting of the American Political Science Association, Boston Marriot Copley Place, Sheraton Boston & Hyner Convention Center, Boston, Massachusetts, August 28, 2002.

79. Evelin Hust, *Women's Political Representation and Empowerment in India — A Million Indiras Now?,* New Delhi: Manohar Publishers & Distributors, 2005.
80. Isabelle Allane and Jacques Verson (eds), *Gender Discriminations Among Young Children in Asia,* Pondicherry: French Institute of Pondicherry & Centre Population et Development, Department of Social Sciences, 2005.
81. Pitam Singh and J.K. Pundir, "Women Legislators in UP: Background, Emergence and Role", *Economic and Political Weekly,* March 9, 2002.
82. Jean Drage, *Women in Local Government in Asia and the Pacific: A Comparative Analysis of thirteen countries,* Phitsanulok: United Nations, Economic and Social Commission for Asia and the Pacific, 2001.
83. Ishrat Shamin and Ranjana Kumari, *Gender and Local Governance: A New Discourse in Development,* Report Submitted to South Asia Network of Economic Research Institutes, Submitted by Centre for Women and Children Studies, Dhaka, Bangladesh and Centre for Social Research, New Delhi: India, Nov, 2002.
84. B.R. Sharma and Manisha Gupta, "Gender Based Violence in India — A never Ending Phenomenon," *Journal of International Women's Studies,* Vol.6, No.1, No, 2004.
85. Asian Development Bank, *Gender and Governance Issues in Local Government: Regional Report of Technical Assistance in Bangladesh,* Nepal and Pakistan, Manila: Asian Development Bank, 2004.
86. Sarala Gopalan, *A Situational Analysis of Women and Girls in Tamil Nadu,* New Delhi: National Commission for Women, 2005.
87. Pippa Norris and Joni Lovenduski, "Blair's Babes: Critical Mass Theory, Gender and Legislative Life" paper for the women and public policy weekly seminar, 1.00-2.30, Friday 28th Sep 2001, Fainsod Room, Kennedy School of Government.
88. Drude Dahlerup, "Using quotas to increase women's political representation", in Karam, Azza (ed), *Women in Parliament: Beyond Numbers,* Stockholm: The International Institute for Democracy and Electoral Assistance, 1998.
89. *Ibid.*
90. Sumedha Sharma, "Women's ways of Governance", *Participation and Governance,* 7:19, 2000.
91. G. Palanithurai, "Role of Elected Women Representatives in Evolving Alternative Governance at Grassroots", *Social Change and Development,* Vol.3, July 2005.
92. *Ibid.*
93. *Ibid.*
94. *Ibid.*
95. J. Jackquette, "Women in Power: From Tokenism to Critical Mass", *Foreign Policy,* Fall 1997.
96. Amartya Sen, *Development As Freedom,* New Delhi: Oxford University Press, 2005.

97. *Ibid.*
98. Jean Dreze and Amartya Sen, *India: Development and Participation,* New Delhi: Oxford University Press, 2002.
99. Amartya Sen, *The Argumentative Indian: Writings on Indian History,* Culture and identity, London: Allen Lane an Imprint of Penguin Books, 2005.
100. Amartya Sen, *Inequality re-examined,* New Delhi: Oxford University Press, 2002.

2

Status of Women and Overview of Decentralized Governance with Special Reference to Tamil Nadu

Status of Women

There is no doubt that the Constitution contemplates a social revolution, brought about through the use of law as an instrument of directed social change. The attainment of equality for status for women was one of the specific objectives implicit in the preamble, the fundamental rights, and the directive principles of state policy.[1] The heterogeneous nature of Indian society with economic and social inequalities influences the status of women. In spite of several measures women's status in India remains in a deprived condition.

Mahatma Gandhi, a great crusader for the emancipation of women in India, wrote, "I am uncompromising in the matter of women's rights. In my opinion she should labour under no legal difficulty not suffered by men. They can no longer be treated as dolls or slaves without the social body remaining in a condition of social paralysis... That is why I take every occasion to protest in no uncertain terms that so long as women in India remain ever so little suppressed or do not have same rights India will not make real progress".[2] But the status of women remains pathetic and India is missing 40 to 45 million every year. This is in the enigma of the 'missing women' about which Amartya Sen wrote in the *British Medical Journal* in 1992.

The main culprit would seem to be the comparative neglect of female health and nutrition, especially but not exclusively during childhood. There is indeed considerable direct evidence that female children are neglected in terms of health care hospitalization and even feeding.[3] The report of the Committee on the Status of Women in India criticized the Indian state that had failed in its constitutional obligation of not discriminating on the grounds of gender. Several indicators such as decline in sex ratio, maternal mortality rate, improper and unequal health care for women and girl children continue to exist. The social maladies are not seriously addressed by the state.

Generally women's status can be understood by examining their

- access to and control over private assets and resources
- access to public resources
- control over their labour and income
- control over their body—sexuality, reproduction and physical security
- control over physical mobility
- access to and control over political space
- access to and control over intangible resources like information, influence, political clout etc.
- position in law and access to legal structures and remedies.

Analysis on this basis shows that where women have been left out. Right from their birth to death women face series of problems. Empowerment measures have been taken at international and national levels to rescue them from this plight. Empowerment of women is also critical for the development of India because it will enhance both the quality and the quantity of human resources available for development. The second National Family Health Survey (NFHS-2) of India conducted in 1998-99 documented women's empowerment in the country as a whole and in each of the 26 states with 1999 boundaries. Table 2.1 shows the different aspects of women's empowerment and the states' overall rank on women's empowerment derived from the NFHS-2 data.

Table 2.1: States in Alphabetical Order According to Their Rankings on Variables that measure Different Aspects of Women's Empowerment and their Overall Rank on Women's Empowerment Derived from NFHS-2 Data

States	*Ranks on Variables Measuring Evidence (EE) of Empowerment*						*Ranks on Variables Measuring Sources (ESO) of Empowerment*				*Ranks on Variables Measuring Setting (ESE) for Empowerment*						*Total Empower ment Rank*
	EE 1	*EE2*	*EE3*	*EE4*	*EE 5*	*Total EE Rank*	*ESO 1*	*ESO 2*	*ESO 3*	*Total Eso Rank*	*ESE 1*	*ESE 2*	*ESE 3*	*ESE 4*	*ESE 5*	*Total Ese Rank*	
Andhra Pradesh	16	20	22	19	10	18	21	10	11	17	22	18	18	20	21	24	20
Arunachal Pradesh	5	5	12	7	5	3	18	17	15	18	10	5	20	19	22	15	13
Assam	17	25	16	14	13	19	17	22	21	19	15	16	26	14	10	18	19
Bihar	21	17	8	25	24	23	25	26	24	25	25	23	12	26	23	26	25
Delhi	11	6	1	4	11	7	2	1	4	1	9	9	1	2	9	1	2
Goa	9	1	13	9	7	5	3	2	5	3	1	11	10	4	12	3	3
Gujarat	8	4	6	22	21	9	12	15	19	15	16	15	2	12	2	7	10
Haryana	6	15	5	11	22	10	16	14	20	16	18	14	5	9	6	9	12
Himachal Pradesh	1	13	4	6	17	2	6	4	22	12	12	13	7	6	1	5	6
Jammu & Kashmir	15	26	21	15	15	20	19	12	23	21	14	20	13	21	19	20	21
Karnataka	23	11	10	13	14	16	12	9	13	9	19	21	24	14	18	23	16
Kerala	10	7	15	2	2	8	1	3	7	2	4	24	17	1	3	8	4
Madhya Pradesh	26	18	18	24	25	26	22	21	15	22	26	19	10	23	17	22	23
Maharashtra	22	9	20	21	19	21	14	13	9	14	21	22	14	10	13	17	17
Manipur	12	14	25	5	6	13	6	5	1	5	3	8	8	7	15	6	7

Meghalaya	4	7	24	8	3	6	8	20	11	12	8	2	16	17	25	14	9
Mizoram	3	1	23	1	1	1	4	11	2	4	2	6	9	5	16	3	1
Nagaland	6	21	26	16	16	14	11	18	7	11	5	1	22	10	14	9	14
Orissa	18	21	9	20	20	22	23	24	15	23	17	12	21	18	24	21	22
Punjab	2	11	2	10	18	4	5	6	14	7	6	17	3	3	8	2	5
Rajasthan	24	19	11	26	26	24	26	25	25	26	22	26	4	25	4	18	24
Sikkim	14	10	17	3	8	11	9	8	3	6	7	7	19	22	5	12	8
Tamil Nadu	13	1	19	18	12	12	15	7	5	8	10	3	15	13	26	13	11
Tripura	18	16	7	17	9	15	10	15	9	10	13	4	25	8	7	11	15
Uttar Pradesh	25	24	14	23	23	25	24	23	26	24	24	25	6	24	20	24	26
West Bengal	20	23	3	12	4	16	19	19	15	20	19	10	23	16	11	16	18

Note: States have been ranked on the following.

Evidence of Empowerment Indicators

EE1. Percentage of women who participate in each of the household decisions with the lowest rank going to the state where women are most likely to participate in each of the decisions;

EE2. Percentage of women who do not need permission to go to market and to go to visit friends and relatives, with the lowest rank given to the state where the combined rank on both indicators is the lowest;

EE3. Percentage of women who agree with at least one reason justifying a husband beating his wife, with the lowest rank given to the state where this proportion is the lowest;

EE4. Percentage who say boys and girls should be given the same degree of education with the state with the highest percentage receiving the lowest rank;

EE5. Ratio of percentage of women who are using contraception and have only two daughters (no sons) and the percentage of women who are using contraception and have two sons only (no daughters) with the lowest rank going to the state where this ratio is the highest.

Sources of Empowerment Indicators

ESO1. This indicator is a composite of the percentage of females aged 6 and above who are literate, the percentage of females aged 20 and above who have completed at least high school, and the ratio of the percentage of females to male aged 20 and above who have completed high school, with the lowest overall rank on this indicator going to the state that has the lowest combined rank on each of the three component indicators;

ESO2. Percentage of women regularly exposed to radio, television or cinema/ theatre, with the lowest rank going to the state where this proposition is the highest;

ESO3. This indicator is a composite of three indicators: the percentage of women who are employed, the ratio of women who are earning cash to those who are employed and the percentage of women employed in professional, managerial occupations with the lowest rank going to the state with the lowest combined rank on the three component indicators.

Setting for Empowerment Indicators

ESE1. Median age of marriage, with the state with the highest median age at marriage getting the lowest rank;

ESE2. Percentage of women living in nuclear families with the lowest rank going to the state where women are most likely to reside in nuclear family;

ESE3. Percentage of women who are at least 10 years younger than their husbands with the lowest rank going to the state with the lowest percentage of women in this category;

ESE4. Percentage of couples of whom both husband and wife have been to school and both have had the same number of years of education, with the lowest rank going to the state with the highest proportion of such couples;

ESE5. Percentage of women who have ever experienced violence since age 15 with the lowest rank being given to the state where this percentage is the least.

Apart from institutionalized deprivation crimes against women are increasing at an alarming rate. The increasing use of communal, caste and ethnic identities in the pursuit of political gains is another factor behind the spreading violence.[5] Most crimes against women go unreported. The reasons for this are: attached social stigma, distrust of legal mechanisms, fear of retaliation and so on. Table 2.2 shows the crime rate against women.[6]

Table 2.2 States and Union Territories in Ascending Order of Crime Rate Against Women

Sl. No.	*State*	*Crime Rate*	*Sl. No.*	*State*	*Crime Rate*
Low			*Lower - Middle*		
1.	Lakshadweep	0.00	9.	Goa	50.54
2.	Daman and Diu	17.48	10.	Tamil Nadu	72.03
3.	Nagaland	25.26	11.	Karnataka	74.51
4.	Meghalaya	29.88	12.	Andaman & Nicobar	75.18
5.	Pondicherry	31.83	13.	Uttar Pradesh	77.40
6.	Punjab	35.81	14.	West Bengal	86.77
7.	Bihar	38.98	15.	Gujarat	89.27
8.	Manipur	44.59	16.	Arunachal Pradesh	91.78
Upper — Middle			*High*		
17.	Chandiagarh	92.15	25.	Haryana	119.41
18.	Kerala	95.76	26.	Andhra Pradesh	121.97
19.	Tripura	99.11	27.	Mizoram	127.89
20.	Jammu and Kashmir	101.01	28.	Himachal Pradesh	139.42
21.	Orissa	110.35	29.	Maharashtra	173.81
22.	Dadra and Nagar Haveli	111.02	30.	Delhi	197.14
23.	Sikkim	114.60	31.	Madhya Pradesh	206.97
24.	Assam	118.78	32.	Rajasthan	208.16

Crimes against women in the form of rape, kidnap, abduction, dowry harassment, molestation, sexual harassment, cruelty at home hinder the status of women. Gender issues which affect the well-being of women ultimately reflect in the Human Development of the Nation. The National Human Development Report 2001 says that "the index of gender equality measuring the attainments in human development indicators for females as a proportion of that of males has improved, but only marginally, during the eighties".

At the national level, Gender Equality Index (GEI) increased from 62 per cent in the early eighties to 67.6 per cent in the early nineties. This implies that on an average the attainments of women on human development indicators was only two thirds of those of men. At the state level, gender equality was the highest for Kerala followed by that for Manipur, Meghalaya, Himachal Pradesh and Nagaland in the eighties. Goa and the Union Territories, except for Delhi, had a gender equality higher than the national level. In the nineties, Himachal Pradesh had the highest equality, whereas Bihar was at the bottom and witnessed a decline in absolute terms over the earlier period.

In general, women were better off in the southern India than in the Indo-Gangetic plains comprising mainly the states of Bihar and Uttar Pradesh. States like Tamil Nadu and Andhra Pradesh in the south and Haryana and Jammu and Kashmir in the north have made considerable progress in improving the status of women vis-à-vis men on the human development indicators. States that have done well in improving their female literacy levels are also the ones that have substantially improved their equality.[7]

In India, Tamil Nadu fares reasonably well in terms of indicators such as female literacy, girls enrolment, female life expectancy, and women's access to basic amenities. The maternal mortality rates and total fertility rates are also lower than the national average. Historically, the socialization of women in Tamil Nadu emphasized women's domestic and reproductive roles. A Kurunthokai poem reads, 'men live by action, but women within the precincts of home by their men'. In the Sangam age, women had the freedom of choice of partner and marriage was a contract and not a sacrament. The post-Sangam age marked the introduction of caste division. Rituals turned marriage into a sacrament and severance was not possible. Chastity at marriage became an obsession, widowhood became a punishment through isolation and rituals. The medieval period saw the coming to the forefront of a few women like Karikkal Ammaiyar and Andal who achieved literacy and religious heights. The rise of the bhakti movement provided a liberating space fore some women, but was also the cause for degradation of another set of women, the devadasis. In the later period of the Nayak dynasty, polygamy became a common practice, further lowering the status of women.[8]

British rule weakened some of the cultural norms impeding equitable status of women. In 1821, the first girls school was opened in Chennai. Women were allowed to sit for university examinations for the first time in 1897, through the Madras University. An attempt was made to recruit women teachers. Nevertheless, the percentage of girls or women enrolled in schools and universities remained very low, although Madras recorded a higher percentage of enrolment of girls in schools than other provinces. Around the same period the social justice reform movement led by the reformer 'Periyar' E.V. Ramasami Naicker in Tamil Nadu played an important role in influencing public thought on marriage customs, widow remarriage, child marriage, sati etc. Another influential thinker was Dr. Muthulakshmi Reddi. She played a key role in the passage of the Child Marriage Restraint Act in 1929 and the Devadasi Abolition Bill (introduced in the assembly in 1927 and enacted in 1947). The Women's Indian Association in Chennai led by Dr. Annie Besant also played a key role in the granting of the right to suffrage to women in 1921 by the Madras Legislative Assembly. Dr. Muthulakshmi Reddi was the first woman to sit in the Legislative Council. Women's participation in the freedom struggle also challenged gender norms, albeit within elite groups.[9]

Since then slow progress has been made in all sectors. However, women's status continued to remain low when compared with men. Table 2.3 shows the Gender and Human Development Index in Tamil Nadu across various districts.

Table 2.3 Gender *vs.* Human Development Ranks

Sl. No.	*Districts*	*GDI Value*	*GDI Rank*	*HDI Value*	*HDI Rank*
1.	Chennai	0.776	1	0.757	1
2.	Kancheepuram	0.710	2	0.712	2
3.	Thiruvallur	0.651	13	0.654	12
4.	Cuddalore	0.643	15	0.644	16
5.	Villupuram	0.582	28	0.587	28
6.	Vellore	0.655	11	0.658	11
7.	Thiruvannamalai	0.608	26	0.612	26
8.	Salem	0.625	24	0.626	24
9.	Namakkal	0.631	20	0.636	20
10.	Dharmapuri	0.582	29	0.584	29
11.	Erode	0.656	10	0.658	10
12.	Coimbatore	0.697	5	0.699	5
13.	Nilgiris	0.686	6	0.685	6
14.	Trichy	0.671	7	0.671	7
15.	Karur	0.641	16	0.647	15
16.	Perambalur	0.592	27	0.596	27
17.	Thanjavur	0.629	21	0.630	21
18.	Nagapattinam	0.652	12	0.654	13
19.	Thiruvarur	0.633	19	0.637	19
20.	Pudukkottai	0.615	25	0618	25
21.	Madurai	0.661	8	0.661	8
22.	Theni	0.628	22	0.628	23
23.	Dindigul	0.638	17	0.641	17

Table 2.3—(*Contd.*)

Sl. No.	Districts	GDI Value	GDI Rank	HDI Value	HDI Rank
24.	Ramanathapuram	0.626	23	0.629	22
25.	Virudhunagar	0.649	14	0.651	14
26.	Sivaganga	0.635	18	0.640	18
27.	Tirunelveli	0.656	9	0.658	9
28.	Thoothukudi	0.703	4	0.703	4
29.	Kanyakumari	0.708	3	0.711	3
	State	0.654		0.657	

Source: State Planning Commission, Chennai, 2001.

Except two districts, in all other districts gender related development index remains low when compared with the respective human development index. At the Fourth World Conference on Women, 189 governments committed themselves to "take measures to ensure women's equal access to and full participation in power structures and decision-making" and to "increase women's capacity to participate in decision-making and leadership". To fulfill these strategic objectives, they pledged to take a prime action meant to "establish the goal of gender balance in governmental bodies and committees. They also pledged reforms in public administrative entities, and in the judiciary, including, inter alia setting specific targets and implementing measures to substantially increase the number of women in all governmental and public administration positions. These were all intended to achieve equal representation of women and men, if necessary through positive action, in all governmental and public administration positions".

Five years later when a review was made by the UN's Division for the Advancement for Women (DAW) for the UN General Assembly Special session on Beijing +5, it was found that women continued to be grossly under represented in the higher echelons of decision-making in government, the private sector, the judiciary, the media, and in academic institutions. Regional and international organisations including the United Nations system have similarly failed to achieve gender balance. The stress for the need of gender balance in all institutions, especially political institutions, is made with regard to the inclusion of women's agenda in politics. Since it gives space to exercise power, women can use the power in favour of them, to enhance their status from low to high. But in India access to the political space for women was granted through a constitutional amendment. Otherwise women entering into politics will not be possible.

Decentralized democratic governance through the 73rd Constitutional Amendment Act has widened and deepened democracy. The UNDP Human Development Report 2002[10] states that democratic governance is valuable in its own right. But it can also advance human development for three reasons.

First, enjoying political freedom and participating in the decisions that shape one's life are fundamental human rights: they are part of human development in their own right.

Second, democracy helps protect people from economic and political catastrophes such as famines and descents into chaos. This is no small achievement. Indeed, it can mean the difference between life and death.

Third, democratic governance can trigger a virtuous cycle of development as political freedom empowers people to press for policies that expand social and economic opportunities, and as open debates help communities shape their priorities.

When this democracy is decentralized the result will be more gainful to the development of the nation.

Decentralized Governance in Indian Context

India has been experimenting with decentralized governance practices for quite some time. In the Indian context, decentralization enjoyed a traditional name 'Panchayat'. In pre-British India, both caste and village Panchayats existed. Caste Panchayats were concerned with issues related to *jajmani*, marriage and rituals. village Panchayats consisted of elders of prominent households in a village. They were concerned primarily with adjudicating civil disputes of residents related to rights in land and administering criminal justice".[11]

Mahatma Gandhi was inspired by an idyllic view of village life and village organisation and formulated his ideas as a *sine qua non* for alternative polity of a free India. He observed that India lives in its villages and its development process will start with village and villagers. Gandhi emphasized the supremacy of the people and insisted on people's democracy as sovereignty at the grassroots which he called "Panchayat".

Gandhi says, "My idea of village swaraj (Panchayat) is that it is a complete republic, independent of its neighbours for its vital wants and yet interdependent for many others in which dependence is a necessity. Thus every village's first concern will be to grow its own food crops, and cotton for its cloth. It should have a reserve for its cattle, recreation and playgrounds for its adults and children. Then if there is more land available it will grow useful money crops. The village will maintain a village theatre, school and public hall. It will have its own water works ensuring clean supply, education will be compulsory up to the final basic course. As far as possible every activity will be conducted on cooperative basis. There will be a compulsory service of village guards, who will be selected by rotation from the register maintained by the village. The government of village will be conducted by the Panchayat of 5 persons elected annually by the adult villagers, male and female both possessing minimum prescribed qualifications. These will have all the authority and jurisdiction required. This Panchayat will be legislature, judiciary and executive combined, to operate for its year of office. Any village can become such a republic today without much interference".[12]

His idea was to establish such a society where every individual got maximum freedom and opportunity to develop personality and character. Therefore, he stated that decentralization was essential for true democracy, in which every one can participate in the decision making and implementation processes.[13]

However, Gandhi's plan of decentralization failed to win acceptance in the Constitution of India. Ambedkar, the Chairman of the Drafting Committee of the Constitution of India had a different view of the Indian rural society. He argued in the Constituent Assembly that "village communities have survived surely on a low, on a selfish level. I hold that these village republics have been the ruination of India. I am, therefore, surprised that those who condemn provincialism and communalism should come forward as champions of the village. What is the village, but a sink of localism, a den of ignorance, narrow mindness and communalism".[14]

Although Gandhi looked at the village Panchayat as a mechanism of all kinds of development very few of his followers agreed with such views. Even Pandit Nehru chiefly supported the view of Ambedkar, and maintained that no progress can be made from the village, as villages are backward intellectually and culturally. Gandhi insisted on the inclusion of the Panchayat in the revised draft. He remarked, "It is certainly an omission calling for immediate attention if our independence is to reflect the people's voice. The greater the power of the Panchayat, the better for the people".

Finally, Panchayats gained a provision in the Directive Principles of State Policy, which is not mandatory. Power was given to the state that if the state wants it could empower Panchayats. Article 40 says that 'the state should take steps to organise village Panchayats and endow them with such powers and authority as may be necessary to enable them to function as units of self government'.

Therefore, it is worthy enough to say that the Gandhian tradition in India facilitates decentralized governance.[15] Pandit Nehru also realized the importance of decentralized governance in India when he started leading the nation. He says, "India will progress only, when the people living in villages become politically conscious. The progress of our country is bound up with the progress in our villages. If our villages make a progress, India will become a strong nation and nobody will be able to stop its onward march if you flinch from your determination and get involved in mutual quarrels and petty functions, you will not be able to succeed in your mission".

Prime Minister Nehru inaugurated the Community Development (CD) programme that was launched under the first five year plan of India in the year 1952. Community development was initiated mainly for promoting development in rural India under the bureaucratic system without taking cognizance of Gandhi's idea of Panchayats. During the implementation period it was observed that the goal of community development was not successful because of lack of people's participation. At this point, it was so important to know to what degree this challenge had been met.

A study team was appointed under Balwantrai Mehta in 1957 to examine the conditions for improving economic and social conditions in the rural areas. The committee's view was that without an institute at the village level which could represent the entire community, assume responsibility and provide the necessary leadership, evoke people's initiative and mobilize their voluntary and spontaneous participation for promoting development, real success would not come about at all. The team favoured democratic decentralization through the setting up of Panchayati Raj Institutions.[16] The committee advocated at establishing three-tier Panchayati Raj Systems through out the country through necessary legislation in states and union territories.

Prime Minister Jawaharlal Nehru inaugurated independent India's first Panchayati Raj on 2nd October 1959 in Rajasthan. After long ages it was observed that the Panchayat System suffered from a number of weaknesses and another study team headed by Ashok

Mehta was set up in 1977. The committee viewed that the Panchayati Raj System was not only meant for decentralization of powers and people's participation but it was also supporting rural development and strengthening the planning process at the micro level.

Furthermore, a committee chaired by Dantwala (1978-83) advocated decentralized block level planning since the centralized planning strategy had failed to provide rural employment and ameliorating conditions of the rural poor.

Another committee was set up in 1982 chaired by Hanumanth Rao, which said that unless planning was made from the lower level the desired result might not be achieved. There should be decentralized planning process at the district level and participation of people through democratic institutions for promoting development programmes.

Later the G.V.K. Rao, Committee was set up in 1980, which said that strengthening of Zilla Panchayat (District Panchayat) and District Level Planning as well as a better integration of block and lower planning with lower level Panchayati Raj Institution's (integrating administrative structure with Panchayati Raj Institutions) was essential for rural development. The L.M. Singhvi Committee which was constituted in 1986, at the instance of the Ministry of Rural Development. It recommended the re-establishment of the nearly forgotten Gram Sabha, comprising all the inhabitants of a village and called the embodiment of direct democracy. The committee wanted to vest PRIs with constitutional status and it also suggested the formation of Nyaya Panchayat for a cluster of villages.

The Sarkaria Commission in its report in 1988 did not favour the ideas of the L.M. Singvi Committee to confer constitutional status on the PRIs, but advocated that the power of enacting any law on Panchayats should vest exclusively with the states.

Constitutional Status

The Sixty Fourth Constitution Amendment Bill (1989) sought to make it obligatory for all the states to establish a three-tier system of Panchayats at the village, intermediate and district levels. However, the states having a population of less than 20 lakh would not be obliged to establish Panchayats at the intermediate level. The term of the Panchayats was to be for five years and, in case of dissolution, they were to be reconstituted within six months. Another significant provision was that the election commission was to be responsible for provisions such as the superintendence, direction and control of preparation of electoral rolls and the conduct of elections to the Panchayats. It also directed that all the seats in Panchayats at all levels be filled up by direct elections. However, the state legislature could provide for representation in the Panchayats without voting rights of members of the Legislative Assembly. As nearly as 30 per cent of the total number of seats to be filled by direct election in every Panchayat was to be reserved for women and allotted by rotation to different constituencies in a Panchayat. This Amendment Bill failed to get passed. Of late, the seventy-third and the seventy-fourth Constitutional Amendment Act saw the birth of a new era in decentralized governance in India. Some fundamental principles of the Act are:

1. Panchayats will be the institutions of self-governance.
2. There will be a Gram Sabha at the village Panchayat level comprising all the adult members registered as voters in the Panchayat area.
3. There shall be a three-tier system of Panchayats at village, intermediate block/taluk and district level. Smaller states with population below 20 lakhs will have the option not to have an intermediate level Panchayat.
4. Seats in Panchayats at all the three levels shall be filled by direct election.
5. In all levels seats would be reserved for SCs and STs in proportion to their population.
6. One-third of the total number of seats will be reserved for women at all three levels.
7. Every Panchayat shall have a uniform five year term and elections to constitute new bodies shall be completed before the expiry of the termination the event of dissolution, election will be compulsorily held within six months. The constituted Panchayat will serve for the remaining period of the five year term.
8. An independent election commission will be established in the state for superintendence, direction and control of the electoral process and preparation of electoral rolls.
9. Specific responsibilities will be entrusted to the Panchayats to prepare plans for economic development and social justice

in respect of 29 subjects listed in the eleventh schedule. The 74th amendment provides for a district planning committee to consolidate the plans prepared by the Panchayats and municipalities.

10. The Panchayats will receive adequate funds for carrying out their functions. Grants from state governments will constitute important sources of funding but state government is also expected to assign the revenue of certain taxes to the Panchayat. In some cases, the Panchayat will also be permitted to collect and retain the revenue it raises. The state finance commission will be established to determine the principles on the basis of which adequate financial resources would be ensured for Panchayats.

The inducement behind the 73rd Amendment Act was to make Panchayats as good governance or an effective mechanism for economic development and social justice at grassroots level. This Act has brought forth a genuine spirit of democratic decentralization in the country. The Acts have ushered in change by providing wide- ranging powers and functions to local level constitutional bodies and ordinary people for ensuring participation in planning and implementation for effective and efficient development. The important initiatives have been envisaged for the people's participation are as follows:

- Preparation of plans for economic development and social justice.
- Implementation of schemes for economic development.
- The power and function of Gram Sabha for reservoir of people's power.
- Regular elections to the Panchayats.
- Proportional seat reservation for scheduled castes and tribes and women.

In consonance with the 73rd Amendment Act 1992, different state governments have initiated new Acts on decentralization. Like other states Government of Tamil Nadu also has introduced Tamil Nadu Panchayats Act, 1994 on decentralization. However earlier attempts were made on Panchayats and local governance in Tamil Nadu and they are briefly explained in the following pages.

Panchayati Raj Institutions in Tamil Nadu[17]

The structural pattern of Panchayati Raj adopted in Tamil Nadu and the functional arrangement — constitutional, financial, administrative etc., have undergone several transformations from time to time. Factors leading to the adoption of a particular pattern of Panchayati Raj in Tamil Nadu are traceable more to local conditions than to central directions.

Tamil Nadu has the unique distinction of having the earliest formed Municipal Corporation in the country. In 1688, a Municipality was established at Madras with a Mayor and twelve Aldermen, including several Portuguese and Indians. Much attention was paid in the Madras Presidency to the revival and development of rural local bodies. In 1864, Lord Robert, the Madras Governor, replaced the exploiting local chieftains with a new class of District Collectors. Distinguished Collectors like Lionel Place, Col. Alexander Read, John Hodgsen and Sir Thomas Munro penetrated into the impregnable mysteries of the villages and found by experience that it was possible and advantageous to work through the indigenous institutions, reforming and adapting them to suit their ends. In particular, Thomas Munro, an ardent admirer of the village Panchayat system, attempted to review the system by a series of his resolutions.

With Ripon's revolution on local self-government, a network of local bodies came into existence. The Madras Local Boards Act V of 1884 provided for a three tier self government system consisting of district boards, taluk boards and union boards. The Madras Local Boards Act of 1920 gave an independent status to each class of local boards and eliminated the *ex-officio* official elements. The Madras village Panchayats Act of 1920 was passed with the object of providing for the administration of village by the villagers themselves, thereby developing the system of self-government in the rural areas. By 1920, the foundation for a three-tier system of local government was well laid with the village Panchayat as the basic unit.

Inaugurating the conference of provincial ministers on local self-government in 1948, the then Prime Minister Jawaharlal Nehru observed that "Local Self-Government is and must be the basis of any true system of democracy". The Madras village Panchayats Act of 1950 was enacted in pursuance of this objective. Adult suffrage was introduced by the Madras village Panchayat Act 1950. The seats were reserved for SC/ST and Panchayats were given judicial powers. District Boards were formed. However, only a very little break through was made between 1947 and 1957 when the report of the Balwantrai Mehta Committee was published. The Balwantrai Mehta Committee suggested the integration of the community development programme and the national extension service scheme with a popularly elected democratic decentralized body scheme. This paved the way for the formation of a new three-tier Panchayati Raj—Panchayat at village level, Panchayat Union at the block level and Zilla Parishad at the district level.

While district boards were abolished in 1957, district development councils were set up in all the districts by the District Development Council Act of 1958. The district development councils role was basically advisory in nature with respect of both the local bodies and the government. The Tamil Nadu Panchayats Act 1958 — based on a white paper of 1957 — introduced a number of changes. All Panchayat Presidents were made members of the corresponding Panchayat Union Councils. This provided an organic link between the two tiers. The Inspector of Panchayat was given the power to co-opt at least one woman member to any Panchayat body wherever there was none. In 1981, an amendment was introduced which enabled the Inspector to nominate a woman member to every village Panchayat. Fifteen per cent of the posts of Panchayat Presidents were also to be filled by women.

In 1989, an amendment was introduced to reserve 30 per cent of the total seats at the level of the village Panchayat for women. In 1991, by another amendment it was stated that if women were not elected to these seats, women could be co-opted to ensure 30 per cent representation in the village Panchayats. Depending on the number of village Panchayats in a Panchayat Union, a maximum of five seats were to be filled by women in the Panchayat Union Council. In addition, the collector could nominate a maximum of two women to the Panchayat Union Council.

After independence, elections were held only four times to the local bodies in Tamil Nadu as per the Madras Panchayat Act 1958. The first elections were held in 1960 followed by the second in 1965 and the third in 1970. The next Panchayat election were due in 1975. But they were conducted under some protests. After an interval of 16 years, the fourth Panchayat elections in Tamil Nadu were held in 1986. Again the elections that were due in 1991 were put off due to various reasons. After the enactment of the seventy-third Constitution Amendment Act 1992, the village Panchayat elections in Tamil Nadu were conducted in October 1996 as per the Tamil Nadu Panchayats Act 1994.

Table 2.4 shows the details pertaining to the number of village Panchayats, Panchayat Union and District Panchayats together with the seats reserved for women at all levels of the three-tier system in Tamil Nadu.

Table 2.4: Details of Reservation of Seats and Offices in Panchayati Raj Institutions in Tamil Nadu

No.of Offices by Reservation	*District Panchayats*		*Panchayat Unions*		*Village Panchayats*		*Total*
	Chair Person	*Ward Members*	*Chair Person*	*Ward Members*	*Chair Person*	*Ward Members*	
Total Offices	29	620	385	6,120	12,619	97,512	1,17,285
ST— General	—	3	1	31	71	517	623
ST- Women	—	—	—	11	35	277	323
SC - General	4	79	43	781	1,876	13,046	15,829
SC— Women	2	54	32	504	1,078	6,302	7,972
Women	8	163	107	1,643	3,154	26,264	31,339
General	15	323	202	3,150	6,405	51,106	61,201
						Total	**1,17,285**

Source: State Institute of Rural Development, Tamil Nadu.

Women who occupy the position of decision-making at the grassroots through reservation of seats are expected to bring about changes in the governing process and improve the status of women. A real difference can be made by these women by taking an active role in politics.

REFERENCES

1. The Indian Council of Social Science Research, *Status of Women in India: A Synopsis of the Report of the National Committee on the Status of Women (1971-74),* New Delhi: Allied Publishers Private Limited, 1975.
2. Words of Mahatma Gandhi cited in Pushpa Joshi, *Gandhi on Women,* New Delhi: CWDS, 1988.
3. Amartya Sen, *Development as Freedom,* New Delhi: Oxford University Press, 2005.
4. Cited in Sunita Kishor, Kamala Gupta, "Women's Empowerment in India and its States: Evidence from the NFHS" *Economic and Political Weekly,* Feb 14, 2004.
5. Brinda Karat and Indu Agnihotri, "Violence Against Women", *Sixth National Conference on Women's Studies,* Mysore, May 31-June 3, 1993.
6. Chandan Mukherjee, Preet Rustagi and N.Krishnaji, "Crimes Against Women in India: Analysis of Official Statistics", *Economic and Political Weekly,* October 27, 2001.
7. Planning Commission, *National Human Development Report, 2001,* New Delhi: Planning Commission, Government of India, March 2002.
8. The Government of Tamil Nadu, *Tamil Nadu Human Development Report,* New Delhi: Social Science Press, 2003.
9. *Ibid.*
10. UNDP, *Human Development Report 2002,* New York: Oxford University Press, 2002.
11. HDRC, *Decentralization in India: Challenges and Opportunities,* New Delhi: HDRC, UNDP, 2001.
12. M.K. Gandhi, *Harijan,* 26th July, 1942.
13. Nazrul Md.Islam, *Decentralized Governance and Development: A Gandhian Vision,* Gandhi Prasang, V (2), 2003.
14. Constituent Assembly debates 4th November 1948.
15. James Manor, *The Political Economy of Decentralization,* Washington DC: The World Bank, 1997.
16. The recommendation laid five fundamental principles down, which were (1) there should be a three tier structure of local self-governmental bodies from the village to district level and these bodies should be linked together. (2) There should be a genuine transfer of power and responsibility to the bodies to enable them to discharge their responsibility. (3) Adequate resources should be transferred to those bodies to enable them to discharge their responsibilities. (4) All welfare and development schemes and programmes at these levels should be channeled only through these bodies and (5) The three-tier system should facilitate further devolution dispersal of power and responsibility in the future.
17. S.Saraswathi, *The Madras Panchayat System: A Historical Survey,* Vol.1, Delhi: Impex India, 1973; G.Palanithurai (ed), *Caste Politics and Society*

in Tamil Nadu, Delhi: Kaniskha Publishers, 1994; B.S. Bhargava, and V.Venkatakrishnan, "Panchayati Raj in Tamil Nadu" in G.Palanithurai (ed), *ibid*; M.Arulselvam, *Tamil Nadu Panchayats and Municipal Laws,* Vol.1, Madras: Malathi Publications, 1994; G.Palanithurai, *New Panchayati Raj in Tamil Nadu (with the Act in original),* New Delhi: Concept Publishing Company, 2003.

3

Freedom Enjoyed by Elected Women Representatives in Grassroots Governance

The objectives of the study are mentioned in the first chapter. A chapter is devoted to focus on these objectives. It may be recalled that in the analytical approach, elected women representatives in grassroots governance were expected to perform on the issues affecting women when they enjoy freedom in the form of political freedom, economic facilities, social opportunities, transparency guarantees and protective security. The present chapter analyses the extent of freedom enjoyed by these women. Before examining their level of freedom the profile of the respondents is presented hereunder.

Age

Age is one of the important factors for women in politics. Age not only relates to the physical and mental make-up of an individual but also serves as an index of the individual's experience, awareness and wisdom in general. Traditionally, age is considered an important factor in respect of one's status and prestige, particularly in rural societies; it was once the privilege of the older people to occupy various key positions in the villages.[1] Age is quite significant to a leader for whom both experience and maturity are essential in role performance[2]. All the same, it is also true that, in the context of multi-dimensional problems in the development process and strange inequalities and disparities, only young and energetic representative can deliver potentially. Though the rural leadership still continues to be dominated by the aged, empirical studies indicate that the installation of young leaders is on the increase in Panchayats.[3]

Table 3.1 shows that 27.5 per cent of the respondents belong to the age group of 21-30 years, 53.2 per cent of the respondents are in the age group of 31-40 years, 9.2 per cent are from the age group of 41-50 years, 6.4 per cent are from 51-60 years and only 3.7 per cent are above 60 years of age. The analysis shows that nearly 80 per cent of the respondents belong to the age group of 21-40 years.

Table 3.1: Distribution of the Respondents by Age

Sl. No.	*Age Group (in years)*	*Respondents*	
		Nos.	*Percentage*
1.	21-30	30	27.5
2.	31-40	58	53.2
3.	41-50	10	9.2
4.	51-60	7	6.4
5.	Above 60	4	3.7
	Total	109	100.0

Source: Computed.

Caste

The Indian social system is dominated by castes and their specific status[4]. Caste prescribes one's status and a person knows from birth his position in the social ranking system. In traditional rural societies, leadership has been a monopoly of the high caste Hindus and the big landlords[5]. Therefore caste plays a predominant role in the rural setting. The tradition which fails to share its power with the lower caste now ought to do it because of constitutional compulsion. The interesting factor to be noted in this study is that six women out of 109 respondents contested in general constituencies and the important thing to be taken for consideration is that one woman is from the SC community.

Table 3.2 indicates that 67.9 per cent of the respondents belong to Backward Communities, 25.7 per cent belong to the SC Community, 5.5 per cent are from Most Backward Community and only 0.9 per cent are from the Forward Community.

Table 3.2: Distribution of the Respondents by Caste

Sl. No.	*Caste*	*Respondents*	
		Nos.	*Percentage*
1.	FC	1	0.9
2.	BC	74	67.9
3.	MBC	6	5.5
4.	Scheduled Caste	28	25.7
	Total	109	100.0

Source: Computed.

The power structure in the rural area is dominated by the Backward Community people. Because of reservation SC women tasted the opportunity of power. But women from Forward Community and Most Backward Community are still under the clutches of patriarchy. The reservation of seats has not created any change in their status of power.

Religion

Like caste, religion has its share in the emergence of women in politics. Most of the village Panchayats under study have a predominant Hindu population. Only a few Panchayats have a sizable population of other religions, namely Christianity and Islam.

Table 3.3 shows that 96.3 per cent of the respondents profess the Hindu faith, while 3.7 per cent are Christians and none are Muslims. The Christian respondents have emerged victorious only in villages dominated by Christians. Religion and caste play the same role in determining the victory of the candidates contesting in the election.

Table 3.3: Distribution of the Respondents by Religion

Sl. No.	*Religion*	*Respondents*	
		Nos.	*Percentage*
1.	Hindu	105	96.3
2.	Christian	4	3.7
3.	Muslim	0	0
	Total	109	100.0

Source: Computed.

Education

In any developing society education plays a key role in the sharing of power and shaping of the person who exercises power. Education fosters all-round development in man—body, mind and soul. It is the fundamental basis for effective socio-political participation[6]. It is only education that can synthesize and crystallize values based on social justice and egalitarianism in a pluralistic society like India's[7]. It is an important instrument of political socialization and seeking active participation of the people[8]. Therefore it becomes imperative to analyse the level of education achieved by the respondents.

Table 3.4 classifies the respondents according to their levels of education. Out of 109 respondents 6.4 per cent are illiterate, 24.8 per cent have attended primary school and completed primary education, 45.9 per cent have completed secondary education, 14.7 per cent went to Higher Secondary School and only 8.3 per cent hold a diploma or a degree.

It is apparent that nearly 94 per cent of the respondents are literate and nearly 70 per cent have studied beyond the primary level of education. This finding is supported by the observations of V.B.Athereya[9] and B.N.Ghosh[10].

Table 3.4: Distribution of the Respondents by their Education

Sl. No.	*Level of Education*	*Respondents*	
		Nos.	*Percentage*
1.	Illiterate	7	6.4
2.	Primary	27	24.8
3.	Secondary	50	45.9
4.	Higher Secondary	16	14.7
5.	Diploma/Degree	9	8.3
	Total	109	100.0

Source: Computed.

Marital Status

Marriage is one of the social institutions cutting across religion, caste and culture and it is looked upon as a necessary and holy sacrament.

Marriage is also an important status-giving device[11]. The institution of marriage enlarges the social boundary of an individual. It is a source of personal gratification as well as an extension of social relations and responsibilities[12]. In the process of getting acquaintance with politics marital status helps women in identifying their political roles and in enlarging their support-base. Most of the married women who contested in the election were made to do so because the seat was reserved for women and hence their husbands could not contest.

Table 3.5 shows that 89.9 per cent of the respondents are married, 1.8 per cent are single, 3.7 per cent are separated from their husband but they are not legally divorced and 4.6 per cent are widows.

Table 3.5: Marital Status of the Respondents

Sl. No.	*Marital Status*	*Respondents*	
		Nos.	*Percentage*
1.	Single	2	1.8
2.	Married	98	89.9
3.	Separated	4	3.7
4.	Divorced	0	0
5.	Widowed	5	4.6
	Total	109	100.0

Source: Computed.

Freedom of Elected Women Representatives

The five types of freedom as classified by Amartya Sen as instrumental freedoms tend to contribute to the general capability of a person to live more freely, but they also serve to complement one another.[13] These freedoms are the principal means in one's life, most importantly, these freedoms help the women in politics to achieve the thing they value and substantiate them to achieve their end. The following analysis deals with the level of freedom enjoyed by the elected women representatives. These five freedoms were considered independent variables for the study. However they are interlinked with each and each variable is assigned various indicators.

Political Freedom

Political freedom determines the power enjoyed by the Elected Women Representatives. From the literature reviewed the following were drawn as indicators to measure the level of political freedom.

1. Access to and control over political space.
2. Access to and control over government scheme.
3. Position held in other organisation.
4. Support from ward members/Block/District Panchayat.

Access to and Control Over Political Space

Access is essential for women to make meaningful progress. This involves equality of access to political space. Neglect of women power in our society is perhaps the most important cause of our backwardness.[14] The reservation has created the opportunity for women to use the political space. If women use this opportunity effectively, they can alter the rules and norms governing gender relations in other institutional sites as well—the family, community, market and the state. Control is the ultimate level of equality and empowerment. The balance of power between men and women is equal, and neither party has dominance over the other[15]. When they have access and control, they can make decisions and play an active role in the development process. Before analysing their access to and control over political space, the responsibilities given to the village Panchayats should be taken into account. Onerous responsibilities are given to the village Panchayats and they are listed as obligatory and discretionary functions in Sections 110 and 111 of Tamil Nadu Panchayats Act 1994. The obligatory functions of village Panchayats are:

1. Construction, repair and maintenance of village roads.
2. Construction, repair and maintenance of water works for supply of water for drinking, washing and bathing purposes.
3. Light of public roads and public places in built up areas.
4. Cleaning of disposal of drainage water and its maintenance.
5. Provision of public latrine and arrangements to clean public latrine whether public or private.
6. Opening and maintenance of burial and burning ground.
7. Opening and maintenance of Public Distribution System.

Apart from this, the following discretionary functions are given to village Panchayats:

1. Planting and preservation of trees in the public roads.
2. Lighting in public roads and public places in non-built up areas.
3. Opening and maintenance of public market.
4. Control of fairs and festivals.
5. Opening and maintenance of slaughter houses.
6. Opening and maintenance of reading rooms.
7. Establishment and maintenance of TV sets etc.

Act provides the above said responsibilities to the elected representatives. As for as women are concern before performing these function main factors have to be taken into consideration in order to measure their functioning. The gender discrimination, promulgated by socio-political-economic system have considerable impact on them. It results in their access to and control over political space. The gender discrimination practiced for centuries has incapacitated women that they cannot stand unless a strong system is provided to them[16]. So their access to and control over the political space determine how far they have privileged from the discrimination practice. It was measured by the following means.

1. Their tenure as the village Panchayat president
2. Decision taken to contest in the election
3. Extent of the influence of family members in the decision taken in the village Panchayat
4. Discussion of the issues in governance with the family members
5. Extent of the support from the government etc.

Table 3.6: Distribution of the Respondents Tenure as the village Panchayat Presidents

Sl. No.	*Tenure*	*Respondents*	
		Nos.	*Percentage*
1.	I time	70	64.23
2.	II time	39	35.77
	Total	109	100.0

Source: Computed.

In Tamil Nadu, Panchayat election as per The Tamil Nadu Panchayats Act,1994 were held in 1996 and 2001. The third election is scheduled to be held on October 2006. The respondents of this study were elected during 2001. Among the 109 respondents 35.77 per cent of the respondents were re-elected for second time to the office of village Panchayat as a president. This is a slight exclination in their political career. Another, important point to be considered is, the reservation for women will be under rotation but the Government of Tamil Nadu instead putting the reservation under rotation, made it sustained for another tenure. This was made possible because the federation of elected women representatives submitted their request to the government to sustain the reservation for another tenure so that it will give them another chance.

These women could have learned more in politics because of their second tenure. Otherwise it will not be possible for them to contest in the election if their constituency is not reserved. Moreover, among 112 elected women village Panchayat Presidents in Dindigul District 106 elected women village Panchayat Presidents came from the constituency reserved for women. Other six village Panchayat Presidents constituencies were in the general constituency. This shows their interest is politics and their consistency.

Among the 109 respondents who got elected as the women village Panchayat Presidents only 16.51 per cent decided on their own to contest in the election. The remaining respondents said that their candidature to contest in the election was decided either by their family members, community or political party. Table 3.7 shows their share.

Table 3.7: Distribution of the Respondents' Decision to Contest in the Election

Sl. No.	*Decision Taken*	*Respondents*	
		Nos.	*Percentage*
1.	Decided by themselves	18	16.51
2.	Decided by spouse/family members	70	64.22
3.	Decided by community	16	14.67
4.	Decided by political party	5	4.6
	Total	109	100.0

Source: Computed.

Among the presidents those who have got elected for the second time, 39.21 (53.84 per cent) said they decided to contest for the second time on their own.

If the seats are not reserved for women these women could not have dreamt of contesting in the election and occupying the position of power. This sort of affirmative action is required for bringing women into polities so that their voice can be heard. P. Manimegalai of D.Gudalur village Panchayat said that her husband might have contested in the election if her village Panchayat had been not reserved for women. Her age is 40 and her educational qualification is 10th standard. She belongs to a joint family which did not allow her to complete her school education. When she wanted to work outside, her family members restrained her and warned her that a woman need not go outside for job opportunities in government departments like the police department, so she withdrew from several opportunities. But when their village Panchayat was reserved for women in the local body election, her husband made her contest in the election on his behalf. She stated that as a woman she always responded to the whims and fancies of the males of her family. Even for getting education, their family members deprived her citing the reason that she was a woman. But when their village Panchayat was reserved for women they made her contest on their behalf without seeking her opinion. Anyhow she felt happy that at last a space had been provided for women like her. Table 3.8 shows the response of the elected women representatives. If there is no reservation will they contest in the election?

Table 3.8: Response of the Respondents Whether they will Contest in the Election if it is not Reserved for Women or not

Sl. No.	*Response*	*Respondents*	
		Nos.	*Percentage*
1.	Yes	12	11
2.	No	97	89
	Total	109	100.0

Source: Computed.

Only 11 per cent might have contested among 109 respondents even though there was no reservation. This shows the level of freedom enjoyed by women to enter politics. Either they have to depend on the decision of their family members to contest in the election or they need affirmative action from the state.

After entering the political space most of them cannot function independently. They have to depend on their family members or traditional Panchayat rather than deciding on their own. They are influenced by their decision. Table 3.9 shows that only 19.26 per cent of respondents are free from the influence of their family members or traditional Panchayat.

Table 3.9: Influence on the Decision Taken by the Respondents by their Family Members or Traditional Panchayat

Sl. No.	*Influence*	*Respondents*	
		Nos.	*Percentage*
1.	Yes	21	19.26
2.	No	88	80.74
	Total	109	100.00

Source: Computed.

Access to the political space was ensured by reservation but the analysis of the data shows that these women don't exercise control over the space they acquire. They are influenced by their family members, mostly by men. This shows that they try to make their female family members as their proxy since they could not contest in the election as it is reserved for women. In the case of SC women, the case is even worse as explained in the following:

Ms.Magudeshwari is the President of Periyur Panchayat which was reserved for SC women. When the elders in her Panchayat came to know that the post of village Panchayat President is reserved for SC women, they commanded Magudeshwari to contest in the election. Now she functions as per the direction of the caste Hindus and elders in the Panchayat. They most often influence her on the decision taken in the Panchayat. She said that she cannot do anything against their wish because of being a woman and that too a SC woman. Her destiny is to follow the words of those people who kept her in the position as the Panchayat President.

Table 3.10 shows that out of 109 respondents only 33.02 per cent discuss the issues in governance with their spouse/family members. Others said they don't have any opportunity to discuss the issues in governance since their family members take care of the matters relating to governance.

Table 3.10: Respondents' Discussion with the Family Members on the Issues in Governance

Sl. No.	*Discussion*	*Respondents*	
		Nos.	*Percentage*
1.	Yes	36	33.02
2.	No	83	66.98
	Total	109	100.0

Source: Computed.

Because of the lack of control over the political space, some have got frustrated and been dissatisfied with what they are not able to do in governance. Only 19.26 per cent are satisfied with the present position, as shown in the Table 3.11.

Table 3.11: Respondents' Satisfaction with the Present Position

Sl. No.	*Satisfaction*	*Respondents*	
		Nos.	*Percentage*
1.	Yes	21	19.26
2.	No	88	80.74
	Total	109	100.0

Source: Computed.

Apart from the dominance of the male family members, these women felt that, the Act has provided them only with the functions such as infrastructure building and construction works. There is no scope for social development and issues affecting women also cannot be solved with this power. They are in a position to carry out the functions assigned to them by centre and state government. Article 243 (G) consider them as local self-governing institution. But indeed they have been made as an implementing agent of centre and state sponsoring schemes and lost their identity. Among 109 respondents Table 3.12 indicates that only 8.25 per cent are satisfied with the powers, functions, roles and responsibilities assigned to them. Remaining 91.75 per cent felt that they cannot solve the issues affecting women because of the gender discrimination with the present powers, functions, roles and responsibilities.

Table 3.12: Response of the Satisfaction of Elected Women Representatives Regarding their Power Given to them to Solve the Issues Affecting Women

Sl. No.	*Satisfaction*	*Respondents*	
		Nos.	*Percentage*
1.	Yes	9	8.25
2.	No	100	91.75
	Total	109	100.0

Source: Computed.

Access to and Control Over Government Scheme

Even though Elected Women Representatives act as the agents of the centre and state government sponsored scheme, at minimum level they should have access and control over those schemes. At least they should be aware of the availability of various schemes particularly, schemes available for the welfare of women since they are expected to act for the welfare of women. Secondly, they should be in a position to bring those schemes to their village Panchayat. Generally central and state government doesn't have the practices of acting upon the demand. They used to function on the supply driven mode. To know these aspects respondents were asked some questions and their response is recorded as shown in the Table 3.13.

From Table 3.13 it can be inferred that 82.56 per cent of the respondent are aware about the various schemes available for the welfare of the people. Awareness on government schemes available for welfare of women particularly were known to 64.22 per cent of respondents. But the access to avail the scheme provided by government was enjoyed only by 49.54 per cent of the elected women village Panchayat president where as only 31.19 per cent of the respondents were satisfied with the general quality of services provided by central/state government for the upliftment of women.

Table 3.13: Respondents' Access to and Control Over Government Schemes

Sl. No.	*Content*	*Respondents*					
		Yes		No		Total	
		No.	%	No.	%	No.	%
1.	Awareness on government schemes available for the welfare of the people	90	82.56	19	17.44	109	100
2.	Awareness on government schemes Available for the welfare of women	70	64.22	39	35.78	109	100
3.	Access to avail the scheme provided by the government	54	49.54	55	50.46	109	100
4.	Satisfaction with the general quality of services provided by central/state government for the upliftment of women	34	31.19	75	68.81	109	100

Source: Computed.

Position Held in Other Organisation

The position held by these women in other organisation gives them a sense of protection and enables them to perform better. This gives them freedom to influence others' opinion by participating in discussion and other activities. Table 3.14 shows their position held in various organisations.

Table 3.14: Membership in Organisation

Sl. No.	*Membership of Organisation*	*Respondents*	
		Nos.	*Percentage*
1.	Self Help Groups	61	55.96
2.	Women's Club	4	3.66
3.	Political Party	78	71.55

Source: Computed.

Out of 109 respondents 55.96 per cent are members of Self-Help Group of women. Out of 109 respondents only 3.66 per cent are members of women's club possessed by non-governmental and women's organization. Among the total respondents of 109, 71.55 per cent are members of political party. Even though village Panchayat is free from party polities, many are loyal towards a particular party. Nearly 72 per cent of the respondents belong to an organisation as listed above but only 33.94 per cent of the respondents have influence over the organisation. Table 3.15 shows this.

Table 3.15: Respondents' Influence Over the Organisation they Belong to

Sl. No.	*Influence*	*Respondents*	
		Nos.	*Percentage*
1.	Yes	37	33.94
2.	No	72	66.06
	Total	109	100.0

Source: Computed

Support from Ward Members/Block Panchayat/District Panchayat

In order to perform better Elected Women Representatives need the support of ward members of their respective Panchayat, Block Panchayat and District Panchayat under which their village Panchayat is located. Without the cooperation of ward members, Panchayat president cannot perform any function or pass any resolution. Even though there is no organic linkage between village Panchayat, Block Panchayat and District Panchayat, without the support of the upper two tier, the village Panchayat cannot implement certain government schemes. So their cooperation is mandatory. This also determines their political freedom. With the case of Sathayi this can be understood better.

Ms. Sathayi, a widow, is the President of the Munnilakottai village Panchayat. Her husband's reputation in the field of community service made her as a President. But the ward members often fail to cooperate with her, since in this village atmosphere they were reluctant to work under the control of a woman who is a widow. She also faces hardship through the Block Panchayat. The person who heads the Block Panchayat belongs to a party which is not supported by Sathayi. Therefore she finds it difficult to bring some of the schemes from the

Block Panchayat to her Panchayat. She said that cultural moorings and her affiliation with the political party serve as an obstacle in her path. Table 3.16 shows the support enjoyed by elected women representatives from ward members, Block Panchayat members, District Panchayat members and officers. Officers have an upper hand over the village Panchayat president.

Table 3.16: Respondents' Support from Ward Members / Block Panchayat and District Panchayat Members and Officers

Sl. No.	*Support*	*Respondents*					
		Yes		No		Total	
		No	%	No	%	No	%
1.	Support from Ward Members/Block Panchayat/ District Panchayat	55	50.45	54	49.55	109	100
2.	Support from Officers	41	37.61	68	62.39	109	100

Source: Computed.

From the above tables, it can be understood that elected women representatives enjoy only limited political freedom. Firstly, they don't enjoy enough powers, functions, roles and responsibilities from the Act. Secondly, they don't have control over the political space. Even though they have access through reservation, indeed the space is controlled by family members and officers.

Economic Facilities

Economic facilities determine the financial freedom of Elected Women Representatives. Marxist feminism says that women's subordination to men was made by the property.[17] Men who have access to control over the public space have the right to hold property and they keep property under their control. Women who are resigned to private space do not have control over the property. The right to property is enjoyed only by men and women depend on men and they are subordinated, oppressed and exploited. This subordination doesn't raise their status economically. Moreover, even though the Tamil Nadu Panchayats Act 1994 provides certain tax collecting power to the village Panchayat, that is not sizable enough to meet the needs of the people. So they have to depend on the centre and state government.

The State Finance Commission, which has constitutional sanction can only recommend to the state government regarding the due share to be given to the Panchayats. The recommendation need not be implemented mandatorily. So far the state government of Tamil Nadu has given only 8% of its total revenue to the local bodies. With this meager amount they cannot do major functioning. Moreover Panchayats can enact budgets only upto 1 lakh. If they need more they have to get permission from the state government. This doesn't provide any financial autonomy. In this situation having budget for women alone for their upliftment becomes impossible. Influencing policy, especially by historically subordinated groups like women, requires[18]:

1. A linking of economic governance to political governance.
2. Building the direction for fiscal policy, and fiscal balances, from below, working backwards from ground level plans all the way to the national balance sheet.
3. Reordering the larger picture, the political economy paradigm such that it ushers in a pattern of development, which is rooted in promoting equity gender concerns.

This may be called gender budgeting which aims to remove poverty, especially women's poverty. This focuses on building the space and method which would enable poor women to move themselves out of poverty. To exercise this they need economic facility but the economic facility is hampered by the state government. They are treated as patients by the government officials and they do not have any freedom to spend the amount in accordance with their needs. To quote Amartya Sen in his keynote address on 'Transition to Sustainability in the 21st century', at the Inter-Academy Panel called Sustainability and Freedom on International Issues, Tokyo, May 15, 2000: "we need a vision of mankind not as patients whose interests have to be looked after, but as agents who can do effect things—both individually and jointly. We also have to go beyond the role of human beings specifically as 'consumers' or as 'people with needs', and consider, more broadly, their general role as agents of change who can—given the opportunity—think, assess, evaluate, resolve, inspire, and through these means, reshape the world". They need joint effort to rise from their present status.

As for the functions of village Panchayats a large number of the 29 functions have been shown as assigned to Panchayats but without allocating sufficient finances which in turn has made these institutions less effective in focusing development planning on the basic needs of the people and expanding local resource base for local development. The availability of revenue for the village Panchayats, revenue mobilized through grants given by the centre and state, and are firstly tied to preconceived ideas of the hierarchical order and does not conform to their actual expenditure requirement.

Further, some of the Elected Women Representatives do not even have control over the budget in their home. Those who earn or occupy some position which earns them cash before becoming village Panchayat Presidents have control over the budget at home. However the majority don't enjoy this benefit and they also do not have control over the property they hold. The economic facilities of the Elected Women Representatives are measured by

1. Their previous occupation.
2. Access to and control over assets.
3. Management of budget at home.
4. Ability to create profitable assets in the Panchayat.

Table 3.17 is presented with these indicators.

Table 3.17: Respondents' Economic Facilities

Sl. No.	*Content*	*Respondents*	
		Nos.	*Percentage*
1.	Employed before becoming Panchayat Presidents	35	32.1
2.	Property owned in their name	76	69.72
3.	Control over the property they own	12	11.00
4.	Spouse/family member will act upon their decision regarding monetary usage	2	1.83
5.	Management of budget at home	19	17.43
6.	Created income generating property to the village Panchayat	14	12.84
7.	Satisfied with the finance available to the village Panchayat	10	9.17

Source: Computed..

From the above table it is clear that out of 109 respondents 32.1 per cent are employed, 69.72 per cent hold property in their name, 11 per cent have control over the property they own, only 1.83 per cent of the respondents' family members act upon their decision with regard to spending money, 17.43 per cent manage the budget at home, 12.84 per cent have created income generating property to the village Panchayat and only 9.17 per cent are satisfied with the finance available to the village Panchayat.

Ms. Mariyarajkumari of Thottanoothu village Panchayat, brought a different experience from her Panchayat. In her Panchayat her predecessor had concentrated much on managing common properties by which the Panchayat could earn Rs.30,000 per year. She constructed a community hall with adequate facilities for a marriage hall and fixed an affordable rent, through which the Panchayat now earns a minimum of Rs. 20,000 per year. She has also planted trees which give fruits fetching considerable income. With the support of the community's contribution of Rs.1,00,000 she has created a very big tank and the tank now provides water for irrigation and drinking. Trees were also planted around the tank. With these measures she has raised the income of her Panchayat.

With the finance available there cannot be any special provision made for women. With the pressure of the national and international women's movement as well as other people's struggles, the government felt the need to appear concerned for its citizens. In the hope of countering critiques of its "anti-woman" ideological roots, the central government declared the year 2001-02 the year of empowerment of women. The Ninth Plan document had detailed the measures to be undertaken to facilitate the empowerment of women described as the free exercise of women's rights both within and outside their home, where they are equal partners with men.

The growing gap between women and men is evident from the 2001 census data on declining sex ratio for children up to six years of age as well as the employment and work trends for women. The Ninth Five Year Plan, again under the pressure of women's movement that earmarked funds for women programmes and suggested a 'women's component plan' covering various schemes and programmes of central and state ministries and departments with not less than 30 per cent of the budgetary allocations directed to them. But practically speaking these women in local governance did not enjoy economic facilities and this will surely influence their functioning for the welfare of women.

Elected Women Representatives don't have economic facilities which determine some of their functioning. Moreover to understand the current financial status of the Panchayat it becomes imperative to analyse the State Finance Commission (SFC) recommendations[19]. In accordance with Article 243 (I) of the Constitution of India, the first State Finance Commission in Tamil Nadu was constituted in 1994 to make recommendations on devolution of funds to the Panchayats for five years from 1996-97 to 2001-02. It is to be noted here that the State Finance Commission started its exercise and came to the final stage before it was decided as to what powers and responsibilities have to be given to each and every tier of the three-tier Panchayat system.

The First State Finance Commission submitted its report before the committee which was constituted for making recommendations on entrusting responsibilities to the three-tier Panchayats. The First State Finance Commission made 462 recommendations for both Panchayati Raj Institutions and Urban Local Bodies of which 49 were common to rural and urban local bodies, 107 were related to rural local bodies and 195 were related to taxation and other issues. Of these only 93 recommendations were accepted in principle and 97 recommendations were not accepted by the government. Even for the 93 accepted recommendations, the government did not issue orders. The details are furnished in Table 3.18.

The Second State Finance Commission was constituted on 01.12.1999 to make recommendations on devolution of funds for five years from 2002-2003 to 2007-2008. The State Finance Commission made 260 recommendations for both PRIs and ULB (Urban Local Bodies) of which 60 were accepted in principle as mentioned in the Action Taken Report placed before the legislature. The Second State Finance Commission recommended devolution of 8 per cent from state owned tax resources for the first two years and 9 per cent for the next two years and 10 per cent for last one year. But the government issued orders freezing the devolution of funds at 8 per cent for each year.

When Finance Commissions are constituted a tradition has been established in Tamil Nadu that IAS officials are to be appointed chairpersons. No doubt they have the capacity and capability to perform in the new paradigm. There are other experts in local body finance or public finance and they can also be appointed. With the minimum responsibilities to Panchayats the First State Finance Commission recommended 8 per cent to 12 per cent for a period of five years. But in the Second State Finance Commission, after fixing enormous responsibilities, the recommendation, instead of starting from 12 per cent started from the same 8 per cent. It gives the impression that local bodies are not considered institutions of self-governance.

Table 3.18: The Status of First State Finance Commission Recommendations for Panchayati Raj Institutions

Sl. No.	*Topics*	*Accepted*	*Accepted in Principle only*	*Not Accepted*	*Orders not Paused*	*Under Examination*	*Total*
1.	Taxation & other related service	93	—	97	3	2	195
2.	Civic services	—	—	26	—	—	26
3.	Organisations	1	—	—	8	—	9
4.	Functions	1	—	—	—	—	1
5.	Devolution of functions	1	—	—	—	—	1
6.	Staffing pattern	2	—	2	1	—	5
7.	Human Resource Development	—	9	—	2	—	11
8.	Community Participation	—	—	—	6	—	6
9.	Adequacy of powers	5	—	—	3	—	8
10.	Control system	1	—	—	6	—	7
11.	Mechanism for performance	2	—	—	2	—	4
12.	Data base	4	—	—	2	—	6
13.	Devolution of funds	22	—	—	—	—	22
14.	Capital fund	—	—	1	—	—	1
	Total	132	9	126	33	2	302

Source: Status of Financial Devolution to Panchayats in Tamil Nadu, G. Palanithurai.

The government has not passed any orders on the recommendations of the Second State Finance Commission. Without economic facilities, it will be a distant dream and a long way for the Elected Representatives in grassroots governance to make their institution self-governing institutions. Further the job will be difficult for women since they have more responsibility to perform for the welfare of women.

Social Opportunities

Social opportunities refer to the arrangements that society makes for education, health care and so on which influence the individual's substantial freedom to live better. These facilities are important not only for the conduct of private lives (such as living a healthy life and avoiding preventable morbidity and premature mortality), but also for more effective participation in economic and political activities[20]. Therefore social opportunities available for women leaders gain them confidence to act in the political space. It is important to them at least in five distinct ways[21]:

(i) Intrinsic importance,
(ii) Instrumental personal roles,
(iii) Instrumental social roles,
(iv) Instrumental process roles, and
(v) Empowerment and distributive roles.

Social opportunity gives direct importance to a person's effective freedom, in terms of fulfilling aspirations for enlightenment, self-improvement and social interaction. It also helps them to improve themselves personally by making themselves aware of many things especially participating in local politics. It helps them to identify themselves with society by participating in public discussion of social needs and encourages informed collective demands. It also gives them instrumental process roles which aim at objectives to be achieved and broadens their horizons. Empowerment and distributive roles contribute to the reduction of gender-based inequalities. The social opportunities availed of by the Elected Women Representatives are classifies as:

1. Education

2. Physical mobility
3. Training
4. Confidence to speak in public
5. Awareness on issues affecting women
6. Negotiating power within family/community
7. Existence of the vision of future
8. Help from family members
9. Respect from community

Education

Even though more than 93 per cent of the total respondents (shown in Table 3.5) are educated, many faced problems in continuing their education. Women getting educated in a rural setup is arduous due to several factors. The significance of education may not be known to the most of the people. Apart from that women in poverty face severe difficulty in getting education. Even though free education is provided, their labour may earn income to the family. Table 3.19 shows that 80.74 per cent of the respondents faced difficulty in continuing their education.

Table 3.19: Difficulty Faced by the Respondents in Continuing their Education

Sl. No.	*Influence*	*Respondents*	
		Nos.	*Percentage*
1.	Yes	88	80.74
2.	No	21	19.26
	Total	109	100

Source: Computed.

Physical Mobility

Women are not allowed to move in public and they are consigned to the private sphere. When women enter polities, their mobility is restricted either because of their family members who often restrict them or if they come out they may face some problem due to the massiveness of evil social movements and of course, their lack of confidence also restricts their physical mobility. Table 3.20 depicts the physical mobility within the village, district, state and India. Out of 109 respondents 96.33 per cent move in their village without any restriction. 84.40 per cent move around their district on their own. 28.44 per cent go any where within the state without any accompanying person. Only 0.19 per cent go anywhere in India on their own without any accompanying persons.

Table 3.20: Physical Mobility of the Respondents

Sl. No.	Physical Mobility	Respondents					
		Yes		No		Total	
		No.	%	No.	%	No.	%
1.	Within Village	105	96.33	4	3.67	109	100
2.	Within District	92	84.40	17	15.60	109	100
3.	Within State	31	28.44	78	71.56	109	100
4.	Within India	1	0.91	108	99.09	109	100

Source: Computed.

Training

Training is one of the significant opportunities available to exhibit the necessary skill for governance. Women who are new to politics need training to learn the administrative nuances. Ms.Shanthi, President of Kambiliampatti village Panchayat got elected from a general constituency. Her dynamic personality helped her to climb in the ladder of power. But she said that the complications in the administrative procedure gave her sleepless nights. When she got the opportunity to attend two important training programmes for elected representatives she did not want to miss and attended. The intensive five-day residential training programme given by Gandhigram Rural University helped her to understand the nuances of administration and taught clarity in handling the accounting procedure. She considers training as an important opportunity. Likewise, gender sensitization training makes them aware of the issues affecting women because of the gender discrimination.

Table 3.21 indicates that 90.82 per cent of the respondents attended training programmes sponsored by the government and other institutions. But only 10.09 per cent are gender sensitized from the training. Most of the training programmes concentrate on the accounting procedure and only a few on social development issues and issues affecting women and children.

Table 3.21: Training Attended by the Respondents

Sl. No.	*Training*	*Respondents*					
		Yes		No		Total	
		No.	%	No.	%	No.	%
1.	Training on running village Panchayat administration	99	90.82	10	9.18	109	100
2.	Gender sensitization	11	10.09	98	89.91	109	100

Source: Computed.

Some other social opportunities are measured by calculating the Elected Women Representatives' level of confidence to speak in public, their awareness on issues affecting women, negotiating power within their family, existence of a vision for the future, help from their family members in household activities and respect from the community. Help from the family members boosts them much. The following case amply supports this view.

Ms. Thirumathal, a widow aged 60 of Palappanpatty village Panchayat is an illiterate. She got elected President and her husband did all the work. She was confined to the home as a housewife and looked after agricultural activities. Her husband suddenly died of cardiac failure. She was shocked at his death. As an innocent women, always seeking and following the words of her husband, she was not in a position to manage the affairs of the Panchayat. She wanted to resign her post as President and decided to send her resignation letter. Her son assured her of assistance and explained to her the Panchayat administration. She was very much afraid of taking the position of leadership and felt timid to take up the activities as a widow. But the support from the family members motivated her to attend to the Panchayat work. Within a year she learnt every activity of the Panchayat. It boosted her self confidence. She is always polite and courteous which attracts everyone and in turn all cooperate with her in all activities.

Table 3.22 indicates that only 43.11 per cent of the respondents have confidence to speak in public, 25.68 per cent are aware about the issues affecting women. Only 11 per cent have the negotiating power with their family members, 31.19 per cent have a future vision of excelling in politics or social activities, 22.93 per cent receive help from their family members in performing household activities, because they have to perform a dual role i.e., household activities and Panchayat activities. 41.28 per cent felt that the community respects them and they feel proud of being village Panchayat President.

Table 3.22: Other Social Opportunities Available for the Respondents

Sl. No.	*Social Opportunities*	*Respondents*					
		Yes		No		Total	
		No.	%	No.	%	No.	%
1.	Confidence to speak in public	47	43.11	62	56.89	109	100
2.	Awareness on issues affecting women	28	25.68	81	74.32	109	100
3.	Negotiating power with in family	12	11	97	89	109	100
4.	Existence of the vision of future	34	31.19	75	68.81	109	100
5.	Help from family member in household activities	25	22.93	84	77.07	109	100
6.	Respect from community	45	41.28	64	58.72	109	100

Source: Computed.

Transparency Guarantees

Transparency guarantees deal with the need for openness that people can expect; the freedom to deal with one another under guarantees of disclosure and lucidity. When that trust is seriously violated, the lives of many people may be adversely affected by the lack of openness. Transparency guarantees can thus be an important category of freedom. These guarantees have a clear instrumental role in preventing corruption, financial irresponsibility and underhand dealings[22]. In order to measure the transparency guarantees available for Elected Women Representatives the following indicators were adopted :

1. Access to information,
2. Entitlement to seek redress, and
3. Lack of corruption.

Access to Information

Information provides knowledge base for any action. Therefore, the respondents were asked about the source of information they get. Most of them listen to news and read newspaper but they are not happy with the media, since they don't supply them with the necessary information needed. They don't get necessary information to run the activities of the Panchayat. Official of the block development office have to provide them the necessary information regarding the administration of the Panchayat. Table 3.23 shows the level of access to information of the women village Panchayat Presidents.

Table 3.23: Access to Information of the Respondents

Sl. No.	*Access to Information*	*Respondents*					
		Yes		No		Total	
		No	%	No	%	No	%
1.	Get all information regarding administration of Panchayat	41	37.61	68	62.39	109	100
2.	Government officials provide assistance when they require	48	44.03	61	55.97	109	100
3.	Necessary information from Media	63	57.79	46	42.21	109	100
4.	Satisfied with the information provided by Media	30	27.52	79	72.48	109	100

Source: Computed.

From Table 3.23 it can be understood that 37.61 per cent get all sorts of information regarding the administration of the Panchayat, 44.03 per cent get assistance from government officials regarding any information related to the Panchayat, 57.79 per cent obtain information from the media and only 27.52 per cent of the respondents are happy with the information provided by the media.

Entitlement to Seek Redress

To sort out their grievances, Elected Women Representatives usually approach the government machinery. But they are not happy with the redressal mechanism. Table 3.24 shows that only 25.68 per cent have gone to the redressal mechanism to sort out their grievances. Only 10.09 per cent are happy with the redressal mechanism. 18.34 per cent have made complaints against government officials who do not provide information to them about the administration of the Panchayat.

Table 3.24: Redressal Mechanism

Sl. No.	Content	Respondents					
		Yes		No		Total	
		No.	%	No.	%	No.	%
1.	Gone for redressal	28	25.68	81	74.32	109	100
2.	Happy with the redressal mechanism	11	10.09	98	89.91	109	100
3.	Made complaint against government officers	20	18.34	89	81.66	109	100

Source: Computed.

Prevalence of Corruption

Corruption has spread its wing throughout the administration and it is engulfed. Only 10.09 per cent of the total 109 respondents say that there is no corruption in the administration and feel that transparency is ensured. Others say that the administration can be run only with the help of corruption.

Ms.Thamayanthi of D.Pudukottai village Panchayat had helped destitutes and widows in her Panchayat and provided financial assistance and income generating activities. She stated that women's personal problems are solved among themselves but several welfare schemes implemented by the government for these vulnerable women have not reached them properly and also it takes more time for getting these facilities. The officials ask for various evidences and proofs. To get individual benefits, they have to give bribes too. She took a stand that on any account bribes should not be given for getting schemes to the Panchayats. This inspired the self help groups and they also developed a healthy practice of avoiding giving bribes to the officials. She also said that both the rules and regulations and the people should take stringent action to curb the menace of corruption mostly in the forms of bribes. Table 3.25 shows the details of the prevalence of corruption according to the EWRs.

Table 3.25: Prevalence of Corruption

Sl. No.	*Prevalence of corruption*	*Respondents*	
		Nos.	Percentage
1.	Yes	98	89.91
2.	No	11	10.09
	Total	109	100

Source: Computed.

Protective Security

Protective security is needed to provide a social safety net. The domain of protective security includes institutional arrangements[23]. Since women are new entrants in politics, they face many problems from different social segments and they need some support from the society and the state to cope with those problems. Amidst several problems they have to perform their functions.

Ms.Maruthambal Albert, President of Panchampatti village Panchayat is a good example for this. She is a progressive leader who has a high level of passion for governance. She said that women Panchayat leaders can do wonders but their achievements are unnoticed. Women Panchayat leaders are always watched. There are people to indulge in character assassination. Police cases are registered against her. She is able to withstand all pressure as she has gained confidence through training. One advantage that the women leaders have in the Panchayat is that they have more enemies than men and these enemies are the watchdogs of the Panchayats. Being assertive in nature and affirmative in action, she takes each and every step consciously and once she decides upon her strategy of action she never goes back. The analysis of data shows that they face several problems in different forms as listed in Table 3.26.

73.40 per cent of the respondents are oppressed by the society, 82.57 per cent are dominated by the males of the family, 80.74 per cent suffer from dual role which includes the burden of doing all household work without any support from the family members, 77.99 per cent are dominated by officers, 10.10 per cent suffer at the hands of political parties which want them to do favours, 84.41 per cent succumb to the problem of character assassination which is common to women in public life, 74.32 per cent lack cooperation from their ward members and 41.29 per cent face threats to life because of their certain actions in the Panchayat.

Table 3.26: Problem Faced by the Respondents

Sl. No.	*Problems*	*Respondents*	
		Nos.	*Percentage*
1.	Oppression	80	73.40
2.	Domination by males	90	82.57
3.	Household chores	88	80.74
4.	Official dominance	85	77.99
5.	Political party influence	11	10.10
6.	Character assassination	92	84.41
7.	Lack of cooperation	81	74.32
8.	Threat to life	45	41.29

Source: Computed.

The main sources of the problem for these women in power were also analysed. They face problems mainly from their family, community/caste/ traditional Panchayat, bureaucracy, political party and other evil elements in the society. Table 3.27 indicates that 40.36 per cent face problems from their family, 30.27 per cent from the community, 20.18 per cent from the bureaucracy, 13.76 per cent from political parties and 86.23 per cent from evil social elements.

Table 3.27: Sources of Problem for the Respondents

Sl. No.	*Problems*	*Respondents*	
		Nos.	*Percentage*
1.	Family	44	40.36
2.	Community/caste/traditional Panchayat	33	30.27
3.	Bureaucracy	22	20.18
4.	Political Party	15	13.76
5.	Evil social elements	94	86.23

Source: Computed

It is interesting to note that 40.36 per cent of the problems faced by them are due to their family members. But 83.48 per cent said that their family members support them when they face any problem from outside their family.

In spite of the several problems they face, only 11 per cent have sought legal remedy. This shows that people don't have faith in the legal system which gives delayed judgment and most of the time the judgment doesn't favour the oppressed. Table 3.28 depicts the percentage of respondents who sought the help of the legal system.

Table 3.28: Legal Remedies

Sl. No.	*Legal Remedies*	*Respondents*	
		Nos.	*Percentage*
1.	Yes	12	11
2.	No	97	89

Source: Computed.

Elected Women Representatives affiliated themselves with NGOs and the Federation of Elected Women Representatives and they felt that they give them a sense of protection. About 52.29 per cent have affiliation with NGOs and Elected Women Representatives' Federation and 51.37 per cent felt that they give them a sense of protection and help them most often when they are in trouble. Table 3.29 shows this.

Table 3.29: Affiliation with NGO and EWR Federation

Sl. No.	*Affiliation*	*Respondents*					
		Yes		No		Total	
		No.	%	No.	%	No.	%
1.	Affiliation with NGO and EWR Federation	57	52.29	52	47.71	109	100
2.	Affiliation gives them sense of protection	56	51.37	53	48.63	109	100

Source: Computed.

Development is viewed as expansion of human freedom, and the assessment of development can be made by evaluating the freedom they enjoy. The above analysis shows that women leaders in grassroots governance are entitled to access and enjoy only limited freedom. They have only limited political freedom, economic facilities, social opportunities, transparency guarantees and protective security. This will ultimately affect their functioning. The finings are summarized in the last chapter.

REFERENCES

1. B.S. Bhargava, *Grassroots Leadership: A Study of Leadership in Panchayati Raj Institutions*, New Delhi: Ashish Publishing House, 1979; S.R. Mehta, *Emerging Pattern of Rural Leadership,* New Delhi: Wiley Eastern Private Limited, 1972.
2. B.S. Bhargava, *Emerging Leadership in Panchayati Raj System: A Study in a District of Rajasthan,* Bangalore: Institute of Socio Economic Change, 1977; Dhan Singh Yadhav, *Grassroots Leadership —Jackhod and Deoroda — in Surajgarh Block, District Jhunjuna of Rajasthan,* M.A. Dissertation unpublished, Pilani: Department of Social Studies, B.I.T.S., 1973; N.R. Inamdar, *Functioning of village Panchayats,* Bombay: Popular Prakashan, 1970, N. Patnaik and H.D.Laxminarayan, "Functional Politics in Village India", *Man in India,* Vol.49, No.2, August-September, 1969.
3. D.R. Singh, *Rural Leadership Among Scheduled Castes*, Allahabad: Chugh Publications, 1985.
4. Talcott Parsons, *The Social System*, New York: The Free Press of Glencoe, 1964.
5. M.N. Srinivas, "The Dominant Caste in Rampura", *American Anthropologist,* Vol.61, No.1, 1959; F.G. Bailey, *Caste and the Economic Frontier,* Bombay: Oxford University Press, 1958, D.N. Majumdar *et.al.*, "Inter-caste Tensions" in A.R. Desai, *Rural Sociology in India* (ed), Bombay: Popular Prakashan, 1969; Andre Beteille, *Caste: Old and New*, Bombay: Asia Publishing House, 1969.
6. Mumtaz Alikhan, *Scheduled Caste and their Status in India,* New Delhi: Uppal Publishing House, 1980.
7. S.K. Goyal, "The Study of Scheduled Caste students of College at Eastern U.P", Research Project Sponsored by Indian Council of Social Science Research, New Delhi: 1973-74.
8. Mumtaz Alikhan, *op.cit.*
9. V.B. Athreya and K.S. Rajeswari, *Women's Participation in Panchayati Raj: A Case Study form Tamil Nadu,* Chennai: M.S. Swaminathan Research Foundation, 1998.
10. B.N. Ghosh, *Rural Leadership and Development,* New Delhi: Mohit Publications, 1996.
11. H.S. James, "Marriage as Status Achieving Device", *Sociology and Social Research*, 29 September-October, 1944.
12. K.M. Kapadia, *Marriage and Family in India,* London: Oxford University Press, 1966.

13. Amartya Sen, *Development as Freedom,* New Delhi: Oxford University Press, 2005.
14. A.K. Pandey (ed), *Gender Equality, Development and Women Empowerment*, New Delhi: Institute of Sustainable Development, Lucknow and Anmol Publications Pvt. Ltd, 2003.
15. B. Suguna, "Women's Empowerment: Concept and Framework", *Social Welfare*, December, 2001.
16. Kiran Saxena (ed), *Women and Politics*, New Delhi: Gyan Publishing House, 2000.
17. Rose Mary Tong, *Feminist Thought: A Comprehensive Introduction,* Sydney: Allen & Urwin, 1998.
18. KWIRC, *Building Budgets from Below — Enabling Women to Direct Fiscal Policy,* Bangalore: Karnataka Women's Information and Resource Centre, 2003.
19. G. Palanithurai, *Status of Financial Devolution to Panchayats in Tamil Nadu,* Gandhigram: Rajiv Gandhi Chair for Panchayati Raj Studies, May 2004.
20. Amartya Sen, *op.cit.*
21. Jean Dreze and Amartya Sen, *India: Development and Participatio*n, New Delhi: Oxford University Press, 2002.
22. Amartya Sen, *op.cit.*
23. *Ibid.*

4

Functioning of Elected Women Representatives on Gender Issues

They dig by the river for brick laying —
labourers from the west country.
Their little girl
keeps scampering to the ghat.
Such scrubbing and scouring
of pots and pans and dishes!
Comes running
a hundred times a day, brass bangles jangling
Clang clang against the brass plates
she cleans.
So busy all day! Her little brother,
bald, mud-daubed, not a stitch on his limbs;
Follows her like a pet, patiently sits
on the high bank, as big sister commands.
Plates against her left side, a full pitcher
on her head,
the girl goes back, the child's hand in her
right hand.
A surrogate of her mother,
bent under her work-load, such a wee
Big sister !

Rabindra Nath Tagore

This poem by Nobel laureate Rabindra Nath Tagore speaks about the responsibility of girl child at a tender age. In the Indian situation the girl child assumes responsibilities from a young age and performs the most difficult tasks with ease. When these girl children grow into women, they perform the same task without participating in public activities. Their activities are confined to the private sphere but the responsibility they bear is great. These functions they perform may be done willingly or unwillingly but they ought to do it.

Women in private life were always made to feel that their household responsibility are precious and they have to do it while other responsibilities, especially in public life, are not their duty. But they can do it if opportunity is given. When the big sisters occupy the political space they are expected to function better than others. The evaluation of anybody's well being can be made by assessing their functioning. In the case of Elected Women Representatives, their actions for the welfare of other women can be represented by their way of functioning.

Amartya Sen's capability approach, which has been adopted in this study, concerns the functioning of Elected Women Representatives. Functioning represents the various things that she manages to do in leading her life. The capability of a person reflects the alternative combinations of functionings the person can achieve, from which he or she can choose one collection. The approach is based on a view of living as a combination of various 'doings and beings', with quality of life to be assessed in terms of the capability to achieve valuable functionings. Some functionings are very elementary, such as being adequately nourished, being in good health etc., and these may be strongly valued by all for obvious reasons. Others may be more complex, but still widely valued, such as achieving self-respect or being socially integrated. Individuals may, however, differ a good deal from each other in the weights they attach to these different functionings.[2] A person's achievement in this respect can be seen as the vector of his or her functioning. The relevant functionings can vary from such elementary things to more complex achievements. The claim is that functionings are constitutive of a person's being, and an evaluation of well being has to take the form of an assessment of these constituent elements.[3]

Closely related to the notion of functionings is that of the capability to function. It represents the various combination of functionings (beings and doings) that the person can achieve. Capability is, thus, a set of vectors of functionings, reflecting the person's freedom to lead one type of life or another. The 'capability set' in the functioning space reflects the person's freedom to choose from possible combinations. The capability set gives us information on the various functioning vectors that are within the reach of a person, and this information is important.[4]

Based on these propositions of Prof. Amartya Sen, the functioning of Elected Women village Panchayat Presidents is analysed in this chapter. When women occupy positions of power, people hope for greater functioning from them. Since women understand the problem of women, they are expected to act upon the issues affecting women. Each may differ in their functioning because the Act provides them with a set of functionings which concentrates more on infrastructure building and scope for development functions. Women who have more freedom as mentioned in the previous chapter can perform functions under eight heads. This can be called the capability set. This was derived from the literature reviewed. Those major functions are classified further as hereunder.

1. *Creating awareness on gender issues*
   - Informing and educating the public about the ill-effects of gender and related issues through folk arts/pamphlets/ notices/ rally/ hoardings
   - Gender sensitization programme
   - Informing women about their rights
2. *Administrative action*
   - Resolution passed in the Gram Sabha to solve gender issues
   - Committee for women
   - Plan for women and girl children development
   - Involving people in activities for the welfare of women
   - Budget allocation for women and girl children
3. *Services provided for women*
   - Water
   - Health care
   - Sanitation
   - Action against liquor
   - Action against atrocities on women
4. *Ensuring women's participation in social and political activities*
   - Making them attend the Gram Sabha
   - Making them participate in the activities of the Panchayat
   - Seeking their help at the time of any issues affecting women
5. *Organising struggle on issues affecting women*
   - Bringing women together on issues affecting women

- Deciding on common action
- Forging common ideologies

6. *Women development activities*
   - Approaching sectoral departments for women welfare programmes
   - Vocational training for women
   - Assistance to destitute and deserted women
   - Formation and assistance to Self-Help Group women
   - Assistance for marriage/education/maternity benefits
   - Assistance to Scheduled Caste/Scheduled Tribe women
   - Employment opportunity for women
   - Ensuring equal wages for women
   - Eliminating gender disparity in school education
7. *Creating support structure*
   - Building alliance with NGOs/Self-Help Groups/Women organisations
   - Member of Elected Women Representatives Federation
8. *Problem solving mechanism*
   - Legal remedies
   - Negotiation

In order to function for the welfare of women village Panchayat Presidents have to work on these lines. But they face challenges from many fronts. On the whole, two major problems seem to confront women. The first is the issue of poverty, particularly affecting women from economically and socially marginalized groups, and the second is the broader issue of human rights violations affecting all groups of women. At the same time, decentralization or localization of political processes, along with reservation for women and marginalized communities, opened up opportunities for these sections to take part in political processes, influence the allocation of government and community resources in their favour and protect and promote their human rights. However, there are several barriers to women from marginalized sections exercising their powers. Such barriers include the harsh economic realities of women's lives, male resistance to women exercising political power, upper caste resistance to *Dalits* occupying public positions, women's lack of knowledge about the functioning of the Panchayats and their lack of access to literacy, numeracy and other functional skills.[5]

Apart from these constraints, they face several problems structurally. The problems faced by the Elected Women Representatives include the following:[6]

1. Presidents of village Panchayats are not aware of all the rural development programmes and schemes. They know about only a few programmes from officials. Even for a few schemes they are not able to get the full details from the officials.
2. The needs of the people are going on increasing which needs enormous amount of resources. To meet all their requirements there is no comprehensive plan and they have no adequate resources.
3. Employees and teachers working in the purview of Panchayats are not employees of the Panchayats and they are all employees of the government and hence the employees are not accountable to local bodies; as a result schools are not properly managed. Yet the Presidents are made accountable to the people for the proper functioning of the schools in the villages.
4. The capacity of the workers working in rural areas are inadequate to meet the problems in the rural society. Attending to repair works in the street light or motors fixed in overhead tanks is not timely and the technicians cause inordinate delay. Rates for the repairing work are very low and hence nobody turns towards these works. For the purchase of materials for the repairing or replacement, Presidents have no option but to give more money than the market rate. Where they will go for this extra payment? Naturally, they will indulge in corrupt practices. Even if they want to be honest the system will not permit them to be honest.
5. Providing shelter is a major problem in the rural areas. Whether it is providing patta or getting housing scheme Presidents have to face a lot of problems as needs are more and available resources are limited. Moreover while providing these facilities the discretion of officials plays an important role rather than the procedures of the programmes and schemes.

6. Selection of beneficiaries for development programmes is a major problem due to the interference of the politicians, MLAs and MPs.
7. Getting the village map from the revenue officials is very difficult because a large number of irregularities have been committed by the revenue officials in the matter of common properties. Absolutely there is no co-operation from the revenue department and other sectoral departments in this regard.
8. It is very difficult to remove encroachments from the common properties. It requires the support of the revenue department and the police. As per the government order they have to support the Panchayat to remove all encroachments on common properties. It is unfortunate that officials are not co-operating with the Panchayats for eviction.
9. Common property resources have not been maintained well to yield income to Panchayats since they are not under the control of the local bodies. They are being encroached upon by influential individuals.
10. Needs are unmet even after the Panchayats came into being.
11. There is no relationship between the needs and the schemes.
12. Still administrative procedures are complicated at the lower level.
13. It is difficult to provide employment opportunities to the needy.
14. Officials' domination over the elected leaders is evident and they dictate terms to the leaders.
15. People's mind-set is that everything has to be done by the government. People are only to receive. They expect each and every thing to be taken care of by the local body leaders.
16. Common property resource management should be given to local bodies. Sand, quarry and other natural resources are the properties of the community. But now by a single order they are taken way from the people without getting the consent of the community.
17. The powers of the Union Engineer (UE) are unlimited and the UE is the embodiment of corruption. He is more powerful

than the Block Development Officer. He is the person responsible for clearing bills, proposals and hence he makes the Gram Panchayat Presidents dance to his tune.

18. The interference of MPs and MLAs in the affairs of local bodies is more and their words are respected and their interference in the local body affairs disturbs the activities of the local bodies. Increasing the interference of MLAs and MPs will kill the local bodies.
19. In all government functions organised in the rural areas, the concerned MP and MLA are invited but the local body leaders are not respected and invited.
20. Presidents are elected by the people and Vice-Presidents of village Panchayats are elected by the Ward Members. But to sign the cheque, it was mandatory that Vice-President should also sign. It disturbs the atmosphere and the administration. The Vice-President demands money to sign (Recently much attention has been paid to this problem and there is proposal to remove this power from the Vice-President).
21. Women Presidents are not respected by the officials. Sometimes they are ill-treated in the offices. They face a lot of problems in the offices of the government.
22. Government orders are not properly circulated among the local body leaders.
23. MPs, MLAs, District Panchayat members, Block Panchayat members are operating funds to execute certain works in the villages without the knowledge of the people and the village Panchayats. All these works are to be integrated. Now these works are not done on the basis of need and hence a lot of money is being wasted by allotting them for construction work.
24. Panchayats are advised to take up works without claiming any advance. Where do they find money for the work? Even after completing the work the Presidents have to move from pillar to post to get their money from the offices for which they have to give bribes to officials at all levels.

This shows that their freedom is curtailed in all aspects and their functioning amidst such a situation is an arduous task. That apart, their functioning for the welfare women and on gender issues will be limited. The data collected from the women village Panchayat Presidents on their functioning are presented in the following pages.

Creating Awareness on Gender Issues

Every society prescribes different norms for girls and boys, women and men, which determine almost every aspect of their lives and their future.[7] This is not based on their sex but because of gender, which constructs and expects difference between men and women. According to Mies, "male-ness and female-ness are not biological givens, but rather the result of a long historical process. In each historic epoch male-ness and female-ness are differently defined, the definition depending on the principal mode of production in those epochs. This means that the organic differences between women and men are differently interpreted and valued, according to the dominant form of appropriation of natural matter for the satisfaction of human needs. Therefore, men and women develop a qualitatively different relationship to their own bodies. Thus in matristic societies, female-ness was interpreted as the social paradigm of all productivity, as the main active principle in the production of life.

All women were defined as 'mothers'. But 'mothers' then had a different meaning. Under capitalist conditions all women are socially defined as housewives (all men as breadwinners), and motherhood has become part and parcel of this housewife-syndrome. The distinction between the earlier, matristic definition of female-ness and the modern one is that the latter has been emptied of all active, creative, productive (i.e., human) qualities".[8] This deprived position leads to various types of issues affecting women in particular and hinders the development of the nation. In the Indian situation, which perpetuates patriarchy from generation to generation through the socialization process no one pays much regard to gender issues and hence gender inequality is sustained. Here comes the role of women in governance. Here, women's agency can play a role in removing the iniquities that depress the well-being of women.

In many parts of the country, gender inequality takes the savage form of unusually high mortality rates of women and a consequent preponderance of men in the total population. This contrasts particularly sharply with the preponderance of women found in societies with little or no gender bias in health care and nutrition. It has been widely observed that, given similar health care and nutrition, women tend typically to have lower age-specific mortality rates than men. Even within the demographic domain, inequality based on the gender can manifest itself in the form of sex-specific abortions aimed at eliminating female foetuses. This natality inequality reflects son preference in a male-dominated society.

The availability of modern techniques to determine the gender of the foetus has made such sex-selective abortion possible and easy, and it has become very common. Apart from these two inequalities, there are other ways in which women can have less than a square deal. For example girls have far less opportunity for schooling than boys; the opportunity to enter polities or commerce may be particularly restricted for women; in terms of employment as well as promotion in work and occupation, women often face much greater handicaps than men.

Inequality in the ownership of property is a classic category of social inequality. This is, of course, the primary factor behind class decisions. While ownership differences between classes and their far-reaching implications have received considerable attention, gender divisions in ownership can also be a source of much social inequality. In many societies the ownership of property, even that of basic assets (such as homes and land), tends to be very asymmetrically divided between men and women. The absence of claims to property can not only reduce the voice of women, it can also make it harder for women to enter and flourish in commercial, economic and social activities. Bina Agarwal has provided a far-reaching investigation of the disempowering effects of landlessness of women in many societies.[9]

The common family tradition in many parts of the world by which men tend to own much of the assets of the household can also be an important factor in the inequality of power within the family. But household inequality has only recently started to receive the attention it deserves. Family arrangements are quite unequal in terms of sharing the burden of household work and child care. While men will naturally work outside the home, it is acceptable for women to do this if and only if they could engage in them in addition to their inescapable and unequally shared household duties. Moreover, one of the most brutal features of gender inequality takes the form of physical violence against women. Violence against women is generally connected with particular social features such as dowry and economic settlements. Even though the numbers involved in violence deaths are dwarfed by the larger numbers that perish from neglect of health care and social attention, the crude and brutal nature of this form of gender inequality makes it a particularly severe manifestation of the deprivation of women.

Women have to come out of the inequalities to have equal benefits of development. The pathetic situation is that most of the women are not even aware of the fact that they are left out and they accept that their deprivation is their fate. Nirmalaganasoudnari, President of Anumantharayankottai, precisely explained the position of women leaders in dealing with these issues. She felt that women have the capability to administer and govern and through this they can change the fate of the whole community. But men are not allowing them to act due to the fear of losing opinion that women lack the mental strengthen and experience for political participation. They also have a crude notion that the public sphere belongs to men. Sometimes this leads to extremely unpleasant harassment of women. She felt that women have a very big role to sensitize men on gender issues. She is doing this among the village Panchayat Presidents. She also keeps sensitizing the husbands of women village Panchayat Presidents who are not allowing their wives to perform their roles and responsibilities.

She said that when the President is a woman, family problems are brought to her notice by women folk and the men mend their behaviour after the advice of the President. Now women have come to discuss their problems as women have come to the public space with the assumption that women leaders will come to their rescue. The status of women will improve if women are made to take up responsibilities in public activities by obligatory or statutory means, she asserted. Therefore awareness should be created among the women to let them know about their condition and position in the society in relation to men. When women occupy a responsible position it becomes imperative for them to act upon women issues. Their first step may be creating awareness in the society about the plight of women. Before acting upon the issues affecting women, the respondents of this study were asked about the causes for women's deprived position in the society. Their opinion is categorized in Table 4.1.

Table 4.1: Respondents' Opinion about the Causes of Women's Deprived Position

	Causes	*Respondents*	
		No.	%
1.	Social norms and culture	24	22.01
2.	Economic backwardness	64	58.71
3.	Politically under represented	33	30.27

Source: Computed.

58.71 per cent of the respondents stated that because of women's economic backwardness, they face most of the problems. They felt that women are exploited and their work is not valued in terms of monetary benefits. 30.27 per cent said that due to under representation in politics, they continue to remain in a pathetic situation. Even though there is reservation at local level, they are not able to make representation in large numbers in parliament and assembly. 22.01 per cent said that, women experience lower position than men because of social norms and culture perpetuated by patriarchy and transmitted by social institutions. After their opinion on the causes of women's deprived position in the society, they were asked how these conditions can be changed. Their answers are presented in Table 4.2.

Table 4.2: Respondents' Opinion on How to Rectify the Causes of Women's Deprived Position

Sl.No.	*Conditions can be changed by*	*Respondents*	
		No.	%
1.	Creating awareness	38	34.86
2.	Improving economic condition	48	44.03
3.	Political representation	28	25.68

Source: Computed.

34.86 per cent said that the situation can be changed by creating awareness in the society. 44.03 per cent wanted to improve the economic condition of women to have a better status for women. 25.68 per cent felt that women's political representation will bring about enormous changes in the society not only at the local level but also at the higher level of governance.

Table 4.3 shows the activities carried out by women village Panchayat Presidents in creating awareness on gender issues in their

Panchayats. From table 4.3 it can be inferred that 30.27 per cent have informed and educated the public about the ill-effects of gender and related issues through folk arts/pamphlets/notices/rally/hoardings. 21.10 per cent have conducted gender sensitization programmes in their village Panchayat. 14.67 per cent of the respondents have informed women about their rights by conducting camps and other programmes.

Table 4.3: Creating Awareness on Gender Issues

Sl.No.	*Creating Awareness on Gender Issues*	*Respondents*	
		No.	*%*
1.	Folk arts/pamphlets/notices/rally/hoardings	24	30.27
2.	Gender sensitization programmes	23	21.10
3.	Informing women about their rights	16	14.67

Source: Computed.

Creating awareness will bring about considerable change in the existing situation. Apart from these the following principles[10] should be taken into consideration to bring about gender equality. The responsibility lies not only with the women in governance but also with the state and the society.

- To establish equality between men and women in laws, institutions, representations, access to resources, benefits and control of these benefits and in all spheres of national life.
- To ensure women's security in all spheres of state, society and family.
- To ensure the empowerment of women in the fields of politics, administration and the economy.
- To protect, fulfill and exercise women's human rights.
- To develop women as educated and efficient human resources.
- To free women from the curse of poverty.
- To eliminate discrimination against men and women in social, political and economic life.
- To acknowledge women's contributions in social and economic spheres.
- To eradicate all forms of oppression of women and girls.

- To take adequate measures to ensure women's health and nutrition.
- To ensure the priority of women in the arrangement of housing which is suitable for women.
- To reflect a gender perspective in the mass media by projecting a positive image of women.
- To provide support services for the advancement of women.
- To direct policy goals to achieve different levels of empowerment.
- To ensure the equal participation of women in the development cycle.
- To uphold and abide by all international conventions that call for women empowerment and achieving equality between women and men.
- To abide by the Constitution that calls for non-discrimination on the basis of sex and scrutinize those laws, procedures or practices that contain manifest or latent discrimination so as to abolish them.
- To encourage and support all strategies, programmes and projects that would lead to the achievement of the above stated issues.
- To allocate new resources, transfer other resources and seek more of international resources for the sake of achieving these policies, whether these resources be material, knowledge, human and others.
- To work in harmony with others and allow the freedom stated in the Constitution for all other parties and partners of civil society and international bodies that would like to contribute to achieving the policy.

The United Nations Millennium Development Goals[11] (MDG) aims at creating a gender equal society, free from health hazard, poverty and offering a wider opportunity for development. The signatories to the MDGs should adopt gender based policies to bring about equality in the society. For this, the primary responsibility lies with the state. The government should devolve powers to the local bodies in order to achieve this. Moreover, the opportunity provided to women in governance should be enlarged in order to take care of the welfare of women in particular.

Administrative Action

Certain functions can be performed through administrative action by Elected Women Representatives to remove gender issues. village Panchayat are blessed with the provision of the Gram Sabha. As per the rules issued under the Tamil Nadu Panchayats Act, 1994 the Gram Sabha can perform the following:

- Approval of the village plan;
- Approval of village budget for the year;
- Approval of audit report on the village Panchayat accounts of the previous year;
- Review of the progress of all the schemes entrusted to the village Panchayats (Section 3 of the Tamil Nadu Panchayats Act, 1994);
- Approval of the beneficiaries selected and location of institutions and community facilities identified by the village Panchayat;
- Review of the completed works executed in the previous year by the village Panchayat and scrutiny of the list of works undertaken in the year by the village Panchayat of by any government department and agency;
- Promotion of communal and social harmony among the various scraps of people in the village Panchayat;
- Mobilization of voluntary labour, contribution in cash and kind for community welfare and development programmes; and
- Examining annual statement of accounts and audit report of the village Panchayat.

The Gram Sabha, which provides opportunity for people to participate in governance, can be used as a viable institution to ensure participation, accountability and transparency. But some studuies[12] show that the functional efficiency of the Gram Sabha is minimized. *Firstly*, hierarchical social structure in the form of caste prevents the participation of all sections. *Secondly*, women's participation in the deliberations is low. However, the SHGs revolution has created a significant impact by raising the number of women participants in the Gram Sabha. *Thirdly*, the resolution passed in the Gram Sabha cannot be put into practice due to the paucity of funds and functional deficiencies. *Finally*, the agenda for the proceedings of the Gram Sabha is fixed by the district administration. This is a severe blow to the decentralized people's participating institution. Hence people lack faith in the Gram Sabha.

Amidst such a situation some efforts have been taken by the Elected Women Representatives for the welfare of women. 6.42 per cent have passed resolutions in the Gram Sabha to solve gender issues. At least they have created an opportunity to discuss the issues affecting women publicly. Table 4.4 shows the other administrative actions taken by the respondents regarding gender issues.

Table 4.4: Administrative Actions

Sl.No.	*Administrative Actions*	*Respondents*	
		No.	*%*
1.	Resolution passed in Gram Sabha to solve gender issues	7	6.42
2.	Committee for women	2	1.83
3.	Plan for women and girl children development	6	5.50
4.	Involving people in activities for the welfare of women	38	34.86
5.	Budget allocation for women and girl children	—	—

Source: Computed.

Table 4.4 shows that only 1.83 per cent constituted a committee for women. According to the village Panchayat Act, 1994 village Panchayats are empowered to constitute the following committees to delegate their functions so as to enable them to discharge their functions effectively;

(a) appointment committee;
(b) welfare committee;
(c) public distribution system committee;
(d) agriculture production committee;
(e) works committee; and
(f) education committee.

Later the government order numbered G.O.Ms.No.102/Rural Development Department (C4) 12/7/2005 re-constituted seven committees into five as:

(a) Appointment committee,
(b) Development committee,
(c) Agriculture and water shed committee,
(d) Works committee, and
(e) Education committee.

These standing committees are supposed to perform their role in order to empower people and ensure transparent and accountable administration. But the pathetic situation is that there is no committee for women and also these committees are not able to perform efficiently since they are not accorded any powers and duties.

Table 4.4 also shows that only 5.50 per cent prepared a plan for their village development including the component of women and girl children development. Six village Panchayats, headed by women, prepared village development plans in Dindigul District with the assistance of the Rajiv Gandhi Chair for Panchayati Raj Studies, Gandhigram Rural University, Gandhigram, and The Hunger Project, New Delhi. Those Panchayats are:

Sl.No.	*Name of the Village Panchayat*	*Name of the Block*
1.	Athoor	Athoor
2.	N. Panchampatti	Athoor
3.	Noothulapuram	Nilakkottai
4.	Kodankinayakkanpatti	Nilakkottai
5.	Mullipadi	Dindigul
6.	Adiyanoothu	Dindigul

Arulnayaki, Panchayat President of Mullipadi village Panchayat shared that though she was not well versed with the Panchayati Raj System, she had her own perceptions over the issues of under development. She proposed to do activities under the three important areas, namely:

(a) education;
(b) women development; and
(c) economic development.

She realized that her villagers did not encourage girl children to continue their studies after schooling and most of them have been living in abject poverty. Moreover due to lack of awareness, women failed to make use of several services like pre-natal and post-natal care available in the health centre. They did not have the practice of prompt reporting and registration of pregnancy. They did not adhere to small family norms. She decided to work against these issues and hoped that the village Panchayat would be a suitable place for those activities. But in practice village Panchayat Presidents were asked to carry out the plan, programmes drafted at top level, she complained. Moreover the villagers were also of the opinion that the basic amenities like drinking water supply, roads and other infrastructure facilities had to be carried out by the village Panchayat, she remarked. There are a large number of issues and problems in the rural areas which are not discussed in any public forum and she has decided to discuss all those issues with the people. She is of the opinion that unless the poor, *Dalit* and women are sensitized and conscientised social transformation cannot be achieved. She has a detailed plan for her village Panchayat and wants to fulfill the following in order to develop her Panchayat:[13]

- Enrolling all the children who have completed five years of age in school.
- Ensuring that the enrolled children continue their studies without dropping out.
- Conducting school annual day celebration to enable the students to display their creative potential.
- Providing basic amenities like drinking water, toilet, playing ground and vegetable garden in the school.
- Creating a sanitation and toilet culture among the students.
- Establishing reading rooms to encourage the desire to learn among the villagers and putting to use the Ayyan Thiruvalluvar Library.
- Providing toilet facility and playthings for children in the anganwadi and trimming their nails to ensure hygiene.
- Enrolling all the children who have completed two and a half years of age in the anganwadi and helping them to learn the habit of attending to their personal cleanliness.
- Ensuring the age-specific weight and the general health of

children by providing them with appropriate balanced nutritious meal and ensuring the proper conduct of activities such as providing nutritious flour and noon meal under the integrated child welfare scheme.

- Preventing female infanticide by creating awareness among the villagers.
- Ensuring that all the children receive fully and properly the benefits of the immunization programme.
- Creating an environment free of child labour.
- Adopting measures to prevent child mortality.
- Creating awareness among the people about gender equality.
- Ensuring that all deliveries take place only in hospitals.
- Creating awareness among women about prenatal and postnatal care.
- Helping women to fully receive the benefits of the activities under the post-natal child welfare schemes.
- Helping pregnant women to properly receive benefits such as pre-natal care, medical examination, immunization vaccines, nutritious flour and pregnancy assistance money.
- Providing the required minimum basic facilities in the sub-health centre
- Helping the village health nurse to discharge her welfare functions well.
- Taking steps to ensure optimum utilization of the women's sanitary complexes.
- Ensuring that all the people get safe drinking water.
- Completely eradicating open air defecation.
- Arranging for common public toilets and their proper use.
- Removing waste in order to create a sanitary village.
- Creating awareness among the people about the dangers to the village from non-degradable substances like plastics and polythene and taking steps for their prohibition.
- Augmenting finances by converting public wastes into fertilizers.
- Planting, rearing and protecting saplings in public places to transform the village into a green village.
- Ensuring minimum basic amenities to all the habitations in the village.

- Installing solar lights on streets.
- Ensuring that all eligible families get ration cards.
- Arranging to issue pattas to those who own no house sites.
- Ensuring that essential commodities are properly available under the public distribution system.
- Building houses for houseless people.
- Eradicating untouchability and creating social harmony.
- Ensuring that the Adi Dravidar community gets all the benefits they are eligible for.
- Organising poor women into Self-Help Groups and helping them to achieve social and economic upliftment.
- Making all the arrangements required to enable the Self-Help Groups to produce articles and to market them.
- Bringing together the village artisans into a federation, enhancing their manual skills and arranging for employment opportunities for them.
- Creating awareness to ensure that girls are married only after they complete twenty one years of age.
- Observing the families of weak, destitute, elderly people, poor widows, poverty stricken artisans and guaranteeing their livelihood.
- Identifying the disabled and reaching to them benefits that ought to reach them.
- Showing the way for male as well as female Self-Help Groups to function robustly.
- Motivating and guiding Self-Help Groups participating fully in public welfare activities and in Gram Sabha meetings.
- Repairing and maintaining water sources such as ponds, tanks, ooranis and kanmois, collecting rainwater in them and using them properly.
- Creating the right perspective among the people regarding the importance of water, water management and utilization of water.
- Developing natural resources and protecting them from damage and degradation.
- Creating awareness among the people to effect changes in agriculture to suit circumstances.
- Creating awareness among the people to cultivate medical

plants in public places in the village and in habitations and to use them.

- Reclaiming common property resources from encroachment.
- Regulating common property resources and taking steps to augment the Panchayat income through them.
- Reorienting the Panchayat activities to a people-centered mode and carrying them out with people's participation.
- Transforming the Panchayat into an arena for people's action.
- Transforming the people into social citizens and making them participate in all Panchayat activities.
- Transforming the Gram Sabha into a forum for social upliftment instead of a forum for collecting grievances.
- Involving women and *Dalits* in a big way in all the activities of the village.
- Synergising the different organisations functioning in the village for development activities.

Apart from these objectives to be fulfilled, these women who have prepared plans for the development of their Panchayats also had specific activities and plans for women and girl children to be carried out with people's participation. They are:

Sl.No.	*Activity*	*Responsibility*	*Methodology*
1.	Enrollment of dropouts (especially girls)	Youth, SHGs, Village Panchayat	Through village education committee the youths and SHG volunteers can assist in counseling the parents of concerned school dropouts and help the dropouts to join the formal school or special school. The Village Panchayat can give special consideration to those families who are very poor, whose dropout wards have been enrolled by extending socio-economic welfare programmes
2.	Proper delivery of RCH services	Youth associations, SHGs, Village Panchayat	Assist in the prompt and timely registration of all pregnancies, ensure proper checkup and follow-up of referral services; assist in availing cash incentive to eligible pregnant women; counseling on small family norm

Sl.No.	*Activity*	*Responsibility*	*Methodology*
3.	Utility and maintenance of women sanitary complex	SHG, women ward members	Counseling of nearby families — forming of users' group — collecting of maintenance fee — maintenance of the complex — awareness building on personal hygiene and environmental sanitation, development of garden in the yard of the complex
4.	Welfare service for the marginalized sector	Youth associations, SHGs, Village Panchayat	Listing poor windows, old age persons, and assisting to avail of welfare; identification of poor who do not possess house site, patta and bring housing scheme to them; identification of physically/mentally disabled and assist to avail of medical checkup for the measurement of the percentage of the disability; assist in availing of eligible rehabilitation services from government and donor agencies; identification of poor women who are not enrolled in SHGs and help them to become SHG members
5.	Promotion of SHG activities	Youth associations, SHGs, Village Panchayat	Establishing good rapport with the concerned NGOs; assisting SHGs to get proper link with various departments and avail of welfare services from the same; assisting to get adequate skills development; assist in the maintenance of SHG building; encourage them to participate in the Gram Sabha; Providing opportunity to be members in standing committees. Involving the SHG members in common activities related to providing of drinking water supply, environmental protection and other social development activities
6.	Welfare of adolescent girls	SHGs, Village Panchayat	Assist in awareness programme on personal hygiene, anemia, AIDS awareness, prevention of child labour, availing of vocational training, counseling them to cautious against exploitation in their workspot

These women have their own perspective for development which includes women in all dimensions. Further Table 4.5 shows that 34.86 per cent of the respondents involve people in the activities for the welfare of women. The process of politically empowering women through reservations in the local elected bodies has helped in the wider mobilization of women. On many occasions they have provided the leadership for collectively organising women to get their legitimate demands fulfilled, like electricity connection and implementation of widow pension.[14] The village women are able to make common cause from the midst of enforced social backwardness.

The Government of India releases more than Rs.2000 crores every year to the rural local bodies to provide infrastructure and it is being spent and yet the people's felt needs are not met as there is no micro level planning at the grassroots which results in waste of funds and improper utilization. The Constitutional Amendment Act and the Tamil Nadu Panchayats Act, Section 243, enjoin that the Panchayats should prepare annual plans to achieve economic development and social justice. This is an important function assigned to them so that the felt needs of the people will be met through such planning. So far planning has not been done at the bottom level. Instead it has been imposed from above. The needs of the people have not been reflected in the planning exercise done above the Panchayats and therefore it was realized at every level as early as 1970 that planning should be done at the grassroots. The District Planning Cell has been constituted and money is being spent for it and yet there is no constant effort to initiate micro level planning as per the mandate.[15] The effort made by these women Panchayat Presidents should be appreciated and they should be helped financially.

But the worst situation is they are not in a position to allocate money for women and girl children in their annual budget due to financial restrictions. The devolution of financial resources to Panchayats is indeed peripheral. Sums retained by state governments in their own hands are mind-boggling. District Rural Development Agencies (DRDAs), which are purely administrative creatures, were set up before the Panchayats became constitutional bodies. They have not been merged with elected Panchayats. Rather, in an affront to the Constitution the Union Rural Development Ministry is spending hundreds of crores annually to strengthen DRDAs administratively with the objective of maintaining them as "distinct from Panchayats".[16] The Panchayats are striving for money to function for genuine causes.

Services Provided to Women

This job is for the women,
To stretch out a thin meal
In a poor country, waters
Needed to complete the deal
Added to precious dal, and
Rice, it makes these grow,
It is the stuff her stick
Fingers knead into dough
These are the tricks she's
Learnt, to eke things out
But when water is scarce
A Woman must go without

Rukmini Bhaya Nair

Women and water are closely related. Several studies show that women are engaged in fetching water most of the time. They have to walk for miles to get water in rural areas. Their primary responsibility in the household chores is to fetch water which is essential for all works and none can live without it. As soon as women came to power in local governance, they concentrated on water and almost all the respondents have worked around water.

Table 4.5 shows that 100 per cent of the respondents have taken measures to provide water to all families in their village Panchayat. This activity saves time for women. Health care and sanitation are other aspects where these elected women concentrate. They don't pay equal attention to their health compared with men and the lack of sanitation facility also leads to several health hazards. So, these Elected Women Representatives worked on these areas. 36.69 per cent of the respondents worked on health care for women. 58.71 per cent of the women leaders provided sanitation facility for women in the form of women sanitary complexes to maintain their dignity. Women are the victims of liquor. This leads to violence and harassment of women.

An interesting case has been analysed to know the extent of the commitment of Elected Women Representatives towards women's health and sanitation. Ms.Kala, President of Noothulapuram Panchayat, has been elected for two consecutive terms in 1996 and

2001. She was educated upto 10th standard and worked as a coolie and balwadi teacher. Realizing the importance of health she properly made use of the opportunity given for the establishment of a primary health centre in the jurisdiction of her village Panchayat. She mobilized public contribution for the purchase of 5 cent land required for the construction of the primary health centre. She has the practice of visiting the PHC periodically. The number of deliveries in the hospital has also increased, she observed. Her earlier experience as a balwadi teacher helped her very much when she became the President. She made use of the balwadi teachers and village health nurse in promoting the health and welfare of women and children. She joined with the nurse in creating awareness among the pregnant women and lactating mothers regarding the intake of nutritionally rich ingredients in their food.

When a women sanitary complex was allotted to her Panchayat, after discussing with ward members, she selected a hamlet of a big size and approached the residents to earmark a suitable site for the construction of a sanitary complex. The residents of the hamlet did not have the mindset to make use of the same. Moreover they were of the opinion that the proposed women sanitary complex should be for away from their habitation. The women did not come forward to give their opinion in this regard in spite of the availability of a woman ward member in that hamlet. As there was no other way, the sanitary complex was constructed at the site identified by the village elders which was far away from the habitation. Women are reluctant to use the toilet. To sensitise the women, Kala, with the help of NSS volunteers of Nilakottai Government Women's College, organised a camp in that hamlet. The girls of the NSS stayed in the village and they used the women sanitary complex. Door to door campaign was carried out to disseminate the importance of personal hygiene and public sanitation. Folk songs and dramas were also staged during the evenings. She said that it is very hard to change the mindset of the villagers with regard to their habit of open air defecation.

The problem of liquor also becomes one of the causes of poverty. Even though illicit liquor was abolished the use of liquor is not completely prohibited by the government. In fact the government runs liquor shops in the name of TASMAC having no care for the plight of women. Most of the rural men who are engaged in coolie work spend most of their money on liquor and leave their family in poverty. So, some of the elected women leaders have organised themselves to fight against liquor and they stopped the entry of liquor shop into their village. 11 per cent of the respondents have done this. Violence against women and girls includes physical, sexual, psychological and economic abuse. It is often known as 'gender-based' violence because it evolves in part from women's subordinate status in society.

Countless daily acts of atrocities and violence create a climate of fear and powerlessness that limits women's freedom of action and controls many of the movements of their lives. The threat of male violence continues to keep women from stepping out from behind the traditional roles that they as women have been taught. Violence and the threat of violence keeps them "in their place". 34.86 per cent of the respondents have taken slight measures to combat this problem.

Table 4.5: Services Provided for Women

Sl. No.	*Services Provided*	*Respondents*	
		No.	*%*
1.	Water	109	100
2.	Health Care	40	36.69
3.	Sanitation	64	58.71
4.	Action against liquor	12	11
5.	Action against atrocities on women	38	34.86

Source: Computed.

Ensuring Women's Participation in Social and Political Activities

Normally women are aware about the issues affecting women but they do not know the ways and means to solve those problems. When they have power and occupy responsible positions they might take some measures to curb menaces affecting women. Even though they are in powerful positions, they may not do it on their own and hence they seek the help of other women so that they might raise their voice collectively. Similarly, in local governance women leaders may ensure women's participation in social and political activities by means of making them attend the Gram Sabha, making them participate in the activities of the Panchayat and seeking their help at the time of any issues affecting women. Self-Help Groups of women help them to a great extent in this regard. They can be easily organised and their strength can be shown.

A case was cited to show the linkage between Elected Women Representatives and SHGs. Pitchaiammal of Kondaninaickenpatty village Panchayat encouraged her women ward members to organise women self help groups in association with NGOs. There are about fifty Self-Help Groups in her village Panchayat. At the initial stage the Self-Help Group members were serious in micro finance rather than venturing into enterprises. After making arrangements for their training with the initiative of Pitchaiammal now they are running small enterprises and several income generating activities. Now these women are attending the Gram Sabha and half of the participants of the Gram Sabha are women. They also organise themselves when any one of their group members is affected and they try to solve the problem on their own. Moreover, they associate themselves with the Panchayat in monitoring the food prepared in the balwadis and schools. She also said that the people of her Panchayat have been relieved to some extent from the clutches of the money lenders who charged abnormal interest because of the micro finance of the SHGs. Further she organised various awareness campaigns regarding law, HIV/AIDS, health, agriculture, and animal husbandry with the help of the women SHG members. Their collective action benefits all. In Tamil Nadu, some of the Elected Women Representatives were already in an SHG. Table 4.6 shows this.

Even though there were no women village Panchayat Presidents from SHGs in Dindigul District, they make SHG women attend the Gram Sabha. Table 4.7 shows that 66.05 per cent of the respondents have made women attend the Gram Sabha and most of them belong to SHGs. 17.43 per cent of the respondents involved them in the activities of the Panchayat. Immunization camps and other such camps were conducted with their participation. 7.33 per cent of the respondents sought the help of SHG and other women during any issues affecting women.

Organising Struggle on Issues Affecting Women

Women in the political field are expected to be activists and organise struggles at the time of crises. In Andhra Pradesh women organised themselves to struggle against illicit liquor and emerged victorious. Their collective action bore fruit. In order to know about their collective action, certain indicators were fixed. Those are listed in Table 4.8.

Table 4.6: Details of Local Body Elected Women Members among SHGs for the Year 2001

Sl. No	*District*	*Panchayat Union Chairman*	*Vice Chairman*	*District Panchayat Chairman*	*Town Panchayat Member*	*Panchayat Union Councillor*	*Panchayat President*
1.	Villupuram			2			2
2.	Charmapuri	1		2			6
3.	Namakkal			1		4	10
4.	Cuddalore						6
5.	Ramnad					2	5
6.	Thiruvarur						
7.	Vellore						9
8.	Madurai			3	1		5
9.	Thiruvallur	1					4
10.	Salem						7
11.	Karur			1	2		
12.	Tuticorin	1					6
13.	Theni						6
14.	Virudhunagar						1
15.	Sivagangai	2	2				
16.	Tirunelveli			1		2	2
17.	Trichy	2				1	3
18.	Thiruvannamalai						5
19.	Pudukkottai			1	1		
20.	Nilgiris					2	
21.	Erode			1			1

Table 4.6—(*Contd.*)

Sl. No	District	Panchayat Union Chairman	Vice Chairman	District Panchayat Chairman	Town Panchayat Member	Panchayat Union Councillor	Panchayat President
22.	Coimbatore						
23.	Kancheepuram			5			
24.	Kanyakumari						6
25.	Perambalur			3	1		4
26.	Tanjore			1		1	2
27.	Nagapattinam						
28.	Dindigul	1				4	
	Total	8	2	21	5	1	90

Table 4.6—*(Contd.)*

Sl. No	*District*	*Panchayat Vice-President*	*Panchayat Member*	*District Panchayat Ward Member*	*Ward Member*	*Town Panchayat*	*Panchayat Ward Member*	*Municipal Ward Member*	*Total*
1.	Villupuram	13	5		99				121
2.	Charmapuri	4	1		49				63
3.	Namakkal	14			85				114
4.	Cuddalore	4	1		69			3	83
5.	Ramnad	12	2		79				100
6.	Thiruvarur								
7.	Vellore	16			171				196
8.	Madurai	13	2		58			1	83
9.	Thiruvallur	15			134				154
10.	Salem	7	2		80				96
11.	Karur				44				47
12.	Tuticorin		17		122				146
13.	Theni	6			104				116
14.	Virudhunagar	11	1		50	2	2		67
15.	Sivagangai	9	2		32				47
16.	Tirunelveli	5			32				42
17.	Trichy	12	2		73				93
18.	Thiruvannamalai	17		1	106			2	131
19.	Pudukkottai	4			27	1			34
20.	Nilgiris				27	1			34
21.	Erode	6			73	10			91

Table 4.6—(*Contd.*)

Sl. No	*District*	*Panchayat Vice-President*	*Panchayat Member*	*District Panchayat Ward Member*	*Ward Member*	*Town Panchayat*	*Panchayat Ward Member*	*Municipal Ward Member*	*Total*
22.	Coimbatore	4	—		44				48
23.	Kancheepuram	19			161				185
24.	Kanyakumari	13		1	129				149
25.	Perambalur	9			118				135
26.	Tanjore	11	2		57	5	3		82
27.	Nagapattinam	11	1	1	61	4	3		81
28.	Dindigul	3		1	64		5		78
	Total	238	38	4	2148	23	13	6	2612

Source: Tamil Nadu Corporation for Development of Women (TNCDW)

Table 4.7: Ensuring Women's Participation in Social and Political Activities

Sl.No.	*Activities*	*Respondents*	
		No.	%
1.	Making women to attend Gram Sabha	72	66.05
2.	Making women to participate in the activities of the Panchayat	19	17.43
3.	Seeking women's help at the time of any issues affecting women	8	7.33

Source: Computed.

Table 4.8: Organising Struggle on Issues Affecting Women

Sl.No.	*Activities*	*Respondents*	
		No.	%
1.	Bringing women together on issues	8	7.33
2.	Deciding upon common action	2	1.83
3.	Forging common ideology	—	—

Source: Computed.

The problems faced by Elected Women village Panchayat Presidents from various fronts viz., family, society and government are manifold. After overcoming those problems they have to work for women. This may frustrate them. Only 7.33 per cent of respondents brought women together on issues which included activities like protesting against the establishment of liquor shop, and atrocities against women on the domestic front. But they couldn't decide upon any common action for these problems affecting women. Only 1.83 per cent of the respondents decided upon common action to be followed by women. These women decided not to cook for their husbands if they drank liquor. Further they could not force any ideology on the whole of the village Panchayat to follow in order to remove issues affecting women.

Women Development Activities

Certain powers, functions and responsibilities are entrusted to the rural local bodies under the 29 subjects which include:

1. Agriculture, including Agricultural Extension

2. Land Improvement Implementation of Land Reforms, Land Consolidation and Soil Conservation
3. Minor Irrigation, Water Management and Watershed Development
4. Animal Husbandry, Dairying and Poverty
5. Fisheries
6. Social Forestry and Farm Forestry
7. Minor Forest Produce
8. Small Scale Industries including Food Processing Industries
9. Khadi, Village and Cottage Industries
10. Rural Housing
11. Drinking Water
12. Fuel and Fodder
13. Roads, Culverts, Bridges, Water ways and other means of communication
14. Rural Electrification including Distribution of Electricity
15. Non-conventional Energy Sources
16. Poverty Alleviation Programme
17. Educational including Primary and Secondary Schools
18. Technical Training and Vocational Education
19. Adult and non-Formal Education
20. Libraries
21. Cultural Activities
22. Markets and Fairs
23. Health and Sanitation, including Hospitals, Primary Health Centres and Dispensaries
24. Family Welfare
25. Women and Child Development
26. Social Welfare, including Welfare of Handicapped and Mentally Retarded
27. Welfare of the Weaker Sections, and in particular, of the Scheduled Castes and Scheduled Tribes
28. Public Distribution System
29. Maintenance of Community Assets

Among these 29 subjects, the activity for women comes under family welfare and women and child development. The powers, functions and responsibilities of village Panchayats are:

Family Welfare

1. Assist in identification of beneficiaries and establishment and maintenance of family welfare centres.
2. Manage and maintain involvement for local bodies and NGOs in family welfare schemes.
3. Implementation of schemes for educating public about family welfare schemes.
4. Implementation of training programmes for family welfare workers.
5. Assist the multi-purpose health workers in the preparation and maintenance of records relating to provision of health care for pregnant women which is one of the components of family welfare programmes.
6. Assist providing proper medical facilities to the pregnant women with the help of the health sub centres in the villages.
7. Assisting of paramedical staff in anti-natal and post-natal care, safe delivery, survival of new born babies.
8. Mobilise the support of the NGOs, and community organisations in extending medical facilities to the pregnant women, and ensure better health of women and children in their areas by improving the basic facilities.
9. Organise awareness campaign among women to emphasize the importance of breast feeding, and its advantages providing in immunity against diseases to the children with the help of the health staff.
10. Assist in controlling the deficiency of vitamin-A, iron and iodine, and arrange for anti-rabies vaccination, and ensure better implementation of the schemes, coordinate with MCH (Maternity and Child Health) staff, village officials and family welfare department by holding periodic revival meetings and ensure integrated efforts.
11. Assist in the conduct of special awareness campaign on sexually transmitted disease (STD) AIDS and killers diseases at village level.
12. Promote Mahalir Mandrams, people's groups etc. and organise awareness campaigns for the benefit of the pregnant women and other women in the re-productive age about anti-natal and post-natal care, small family norms, breast feeding.

Women and Child Development

1. Supervise the meal centres functioning in the village.
2. Supervise the integrated child development scheme/Tamil Nadu Integrated Nutritious Programme (TINP).
3. Implement and supervise the formation of pre-school and crèches, implementation of nutrition schemes in schools and integrated child development programme centres.
4. Assist in starting balwadis and schools.
5. Assist in construction of child welfare centres under Swedish assisted integrated child development programme centres.
6. Assist, supervision and evaluation of nutritional meal scheme.
7. Assist in prevention of female infanticide and development of children and destitute women.
8. Assist and supervise the working women centres and production units.
9. Assist and supervise various women welfare schemes such as vocational training, poor widow's children and daughters marriage assistance and orphanages.
10. Assist in implementing the women related economic development activities.
11. Supervise and review of crèches for children of working and diseased women.
12. Assist for implementation of all women welfare schemes.
13. Assist the pregnant women, below the poverty line to get financial assistance.
14. Assist in getting financial assistance for below women poverty line for marriage.
15. Assist in getting financial assistance to female children.
16. Assist in distributing of serving mechanics to destitute and deserted women.
17. Assist in distribution of advance money to poor widows' daughters marriage.
18. Identify the women and children suffering from anemic, micro-nutrient deficiency (vitamin A, iron and iodine deficiency) goiter and inform it to the social welfare development officials.
19. Assist in implementation of women development under International Fund for Agriculture Development (IFAD) Schemes.

20. Assist the concerned department officials for eligible women who come forward for training and to take up self-employment ventures.
21. Arrange to co-ordinate the women groups with the social welfare department officials in implementation of social welfare schemes and supervise the same.
22. Creating awareness about the schemes implemented by government and disseminate information about clean health habits to be adopted, healthy food habits, breast feeding for improvement of standard of living of women and children living in rural areas.
23. village Panchayats may extend and coordinate the following assistance to the social welfare department officials.
24. Inspect the centres assisted by the government, identify the shortcomings and rectify the defects if any.
25. Enlist the local support in the village for supplying of vegetables and other articles required for the nutritious meal centres.
26. The elected women representatives of village Panchayats can help the social welfare department staff in monitoring of growth of children, pre-natal and post-natal care, child care activities.
27. Assist the project officials for involving the non-governmental organisations.
28. To assist in selection of sites for construction of child welfare centres and nutritious meal centres.
29. To assist in taking census and collect statistics related to women and children for evaluation of schemes.
30. To assist the social welfare department officials in identifying the child labourers and extend the rehabilitation measures for their upliftment by utilizing the various schemes of government.
31. Assist in formation of Self-Help Groups among women and include the habit of small saving among them.

The list of functions is exhaustive but they are provided without any devolution of finance. Likewise, in all these functions they can only assist the government sector and they cannot decide on their own course of action. Only executive orders[17] were passed to the social welfare and nutrition department and health and welfare department. There is no concrete legislative order regarding the devolution of functions to village Panchayats from government departments. However, these Elected Women Representatives have performed certain women development activities. R.K.Renganayaki of Paganatham village Panchayat has performed several activities for women development. When the innovative scheme of 'Namathu Gramam' was introduced in all the village Panchayats of Tamil Nadu, she, with the cooperation of the village undertook activities. She gave attention to the following activities:

- Maximum utilization of women's sanitary complex.
- Cleanliness in streets and lanes
- Segregation of wastes — organic and inorganic
- Tree planting in all houses, public lands, school campus and tanks
- Cent percent school enrollment
- Education of girl children
- Eradication of child labour
- Creating awareness about the age of marriage
- Prevention of female infanticide
- Transparency in Panchayat administration.

Some of the activities performed by EWRs are listed in Table 4.9.

Table 4.9: Women Development Activities of Elected Women Representatives

Sl. No.	*Women Development Activities*	*Respondents*	
		No.	*Percentage*
1.	Approaching sectoral department for women welfare programmes	18	16.51
2.	Vocational training for women	15	13.76
3.	Assistance to destitute and deserted	88	80.73
4.	Formation and assistance to SHG women	40	36.69
5.	Assistance to SC/ST women	35	32.11
6.	Assistance for marriage/education/maternity benefits	71	65.13
7.	Employment opportunity for women	12	11.00
8.	Ensuring equal wages for women	16	14.67
9.	Eliminating gender disparity in school education	68	62.38

Source: Computed.

Many activities in the rural setting will be very difficult for women. The best example to cite is ensuring equal wages for women. Women's productive and reproductive work is generally not assigned much economic value. According to the UNDP Human Development Report of 1995 the invisible and unpaid work contributed by women annually is worth US $11 trillion. This is because of the gender division of labour. Men and women, boys and girls learn and master only those skills considered appropriate to their gender roles. This leads to hierarchies and inequalities, because men and women's labour is not valued or rewarded equally.[18] Women's work is undervalued and they are paid less which may lead to feminization of poverty. At least, 14.67 per cent of women have made an attempt to ensure equal wages for women for their labour on par with men. This will bring about a significant change in the life of women.

Creating Support Structure

Apart from solving the problems of women, these Elected Women Representatives face several problems on their own. Some of them have found a support structure and built an alliance so that they can seek their help and guidance whenever necessary. In turn, this may help them in enhancing their functioning on issues affecting women. Venkateswari, President of Gandhigram village Panchayat, explained the need for creating a support structure and especially the role of the Elected Women Representatives federation. She said that many of the women leaders from Kanyakumari to Chennai have solved their problems through this Federation. She pointed out that when a woman leader was murdered in Urapakkam, no FIR was filed. The FIR was filed only after the intervention of the Federation. There are many Federations, namely, District Panchayat Leaders Federation, Block Panchayat Leaders Federation and village Panchayat Leaders Federation, but they are not visible. It is only the Women's Federation that is invisible by its activities and has proved its efficiency by solving many problems effectively and also acts as a support basis for women who are new entrants to governance. Table 4.10 shows the support structure created by the respondents.

Table 4.10: Support Structure Created by the Respondents

Sl.No.	*Support Structure*	*Respondents*	
		No.	*Percentage*
1.	Building alliance with NGOs/SHG and other Women Organisations	16	14.67
2.	Member of Elected Women Representatives Federation	38	34.86

Source: Computed.

NGOs play a crucial role in mobilizing the masses for development activities in the rural areas. They have a supporting networking system at the grassroots. So these grassroots NGOs will play a commendable role in empowering women and simultaneously associate women leaders at the grassroots level. 14.67 per cent of the respondents built alliance with NGOs/SHG and other women organisations. Similarly Elected Women Representatives Federation will help to address issues for the general cause of women in their functioning. 34.86 per cent of the respondents were members of the Elected Women Representatives Federation.

Problem Solving Mechanism

The problem faced by women are many as discussed earlier and those problems can be solved either through the legal system or through negotiation. But due to the prolonged time taken by the legal system for its judgment and also the loop holes in the legal system the people lose faith in the legal system. Kaviarasi of Javvathupatty village Panchayat said that she often looks into the matter of gender issues in her Panchayat and through negotiation she solves most of the problems. She said that once a middle aged woman knocked at her door at midnight and made a complaint that her husband is battering her all the time out of suspicion and she can't live with him any more. Many advised her to take the matter to the police station. But Kaviarasi said that, if they lodged a complaint in the police station, the case many be prolonged and she wanted to settle the issue amicably. So the next morning she, along with some elders of the village, went to the house of the affected person, made him understand the plight of his wife and warned him severely. If she came to know that he was beating his wife again, she said that she would take stringent action against him by taking his property away and sending him out the village and this was agreed to by all others. She finally said that if it went beyond her control she would take the issue to the police station but added that she did not have faith in our legal system since the proceedings and judgment always affect women psychologically and they are not women friendly at all. 59.63 per cent of the respondents said that they solved most of the problems through negotiation. Only 5.50 per cent said they sought the help of the legal system.

Table 4.11: Problem Solving Mechanism of the Respondents

Sl.No.	*Problem Solving Mechanism*	*Respondents*	
		No.	*Percentage*
1.	Legal System	6	5.50
2.	Negotiation	65	59.63

Source: Computed.

Thus the analysis shows that the functioning of Elected Women Representatives particularly on gender issues is very limited. The capability set offered them is wider but due to lack of freedom they are not in a position to select the functioning from the capability set. The relationship between freedom and functioning is explained in the next chapter.

References

1. Amartya Sen, *Development as Freedom,* New Delhi: Oxford University Press, 2005.
2. Amartya Sen, "Capability and Well-being" in Martha Nussbaum and Amartya Sen (eds), *The Quality of Life,* New Delhi: Oxford University Press, 2000.
3. Amartya Sen, *Inequality reexamined,* New Delhi: Oxford University Press, 2002.
4. *Ibid.*
5. Ranjani K. Murthy (ed), *Building Women's Capacities: Interventions in Gender Transformation,* New Delhi: Sage Publications, 2001.
6. Rajiv Gandhi Chair for Panchayati Raj Studies, Report of the Leadership Training and Capacity Building Exercise Programme for Gram Panchayat Women Leaders in Dindigul District, Gandhigram: Rajiv Gandhi Chair for Panchayati Raj Studies, G. Palanithurai, *New Panchayati Raj System in*

Tamil Nadu (With the Act in Original), New Delhi: Concept Publishing Company, 2003.
7. Kamla Bhasin, *Understanding Gender,* New Delhi: Kali for Women, 2000.
8. Maria Mies, *et.al., Women: The Last Colony,* New Delhi: Kali for Women, 1988.
9. Bina Agarwal, *A Field of One's Own,* Cambridge: Cambridge University Press, 1994.
10. United Nations Development Programme in Collaboration with the National Council for Strategic Planning, Human Development and Millennium Development Goals (MDGs) Goal 3: Promote Gender Equality and Empower Women: Mainstreaming Gender Equality and Women's Empowerment, prepared by Ahfad University of Women, Institute of Women, Gender and Development Studies, Oct, 2003.
11. The Millennium Development Goals are an ambitious agenda for reducing poverty and improving lives, agreed on by world leaders at the Millennium Summit in September 2000 (www.un.org/millennium/summit.html) for each goals as listed below one or more targets have been set, most for 2015, using 1990 as a benchmark.
    (a) Eradicate Extreme Poverty and Hunger
    (b) Achieve Universal Primary Education
    (c) Promote Gender Equality and Empower Women
    (d) Reduce Child Mortality
    (e) Improve Maternal Health
    (f) Combat HIV.AIDS, Malaria and Other Diseases
    (g) Ensure Environmental Sustainability
    (h) Develop a Global Partnership for Development.
12. G. Palanithurai and V. Ragupathy, *Functional Efficiency of Gram Sabha in Tamil Nadu,* New Delhi: Concept Publishing Company, 2005.
13. The detail of the plan can be found in the plan document of those six village Panchayat prepared by the Village Planning Committee.
14. Rinku Pegu, "Putting Her Best Foot Forward", *The Hindu*, dated 04.05.2003.
15. G. Palanithurai, *Status of Financial Devolution to Panchayats in Tamil Nadu,* Gandhigram: Rajiv Gandhi Chair for Panchayati Raj Studies, May 2004.
16. L.C. Jain, "Adding Life to Years", *The Hindu,* dated 11.05.2003.
17. Four executive orders under the subject family welfare and women and child development were passed. They were:
    - G.O. M.S. No.220 Rural Development dated 4.1.97.
    - G.O. M.S. No.274 Health and Welfare dated 8.6.99.
    - G.O. M.S. No.2 Social Welfare and Nutrition Department dated 5.1.99.
    - G.O. M.S. No.110 Social Welfare and Nutrition Department dated 4.6.99.
18. Kamla Bhasin, *Understanding Gender*, New Delhi: Kali for Women, 2000.

5

Relationship Between Freedom Enjoyed by Elected Women Representatives (EWRs) and The Functioning They Manifested on Gender Issues

Political freedom, economic facility, social opportunity, transparency guarantee and protective security enhance the capabilities of people, but they also supplement one another and can furthermore reinforce one another.[1] These freedoms ultimately result in the range of functioning. This chapter analyses the relationship between the freedom enjoyed by the elected women representatives and the functioning they performed on gender issues. The range of functioning of EWRs on gender issues eventually depends mainly on the freedom available and enjoyed by the EWRs. The hypothesis of the study states that "the greater the freedom the EWRs enjoy, greater the functioning the EWRs perform". In order to explore the relationship between the freedom and functioning statistical tools like correlation and regression was used.

The assessment of performance of grassroots leaders for the welfare of women folk is made by calculating the functioning performed by them. But this functioning greatly depends upon the wider range of freedom which was classified under five heads for this study. These different kinds of freedom interrelate with one another and freedom of one type may greatly help in advancing freedom of other types.[2] Moreover, the study identifies the valuable functioning of EWRs on gender issues which may be termed 'capability set'. This set has eight major functionings as discussed earlier and under each head, possible functionings were enumerated. The set of functionings a person is able to achieve to a satisfactory level determines the capability of EWRs. The alternative combination of functioning from the 'capability set' can be termed as functioning verctor.[3] However, in choosing the alternative combinations of various functioning the freedom plays a crucial role. It is only the freedom which determines the ability of a person to determine their way of functioning. The possible functioning for each freedom attained by EWRs can be presented schematically as hereunder:

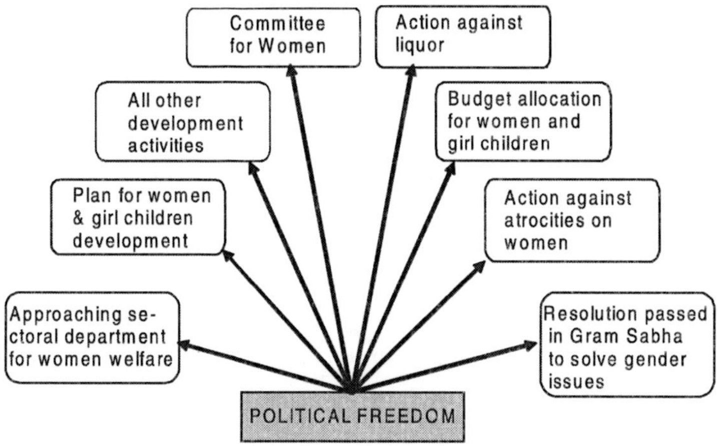

Fig. 5.1: Political Freedom

Testing of Hypothesis

In order to explore the relationship between freedom and functioning correlation and regression analysis were used.

Table 5.1: Correlation Between Freedom and Functioning of EWRs on Gender Issues

Sl. No.	*Freedom*	*Functioning of EWRs on Gender Issues*
1.	Political Freedom	0.505
2.	Economic Facilities	0.464
3.	Social Opportunities	0.397
4.	Transparency Guarantee	0.270
5.	Protective Security	0.422

Source: Computed.

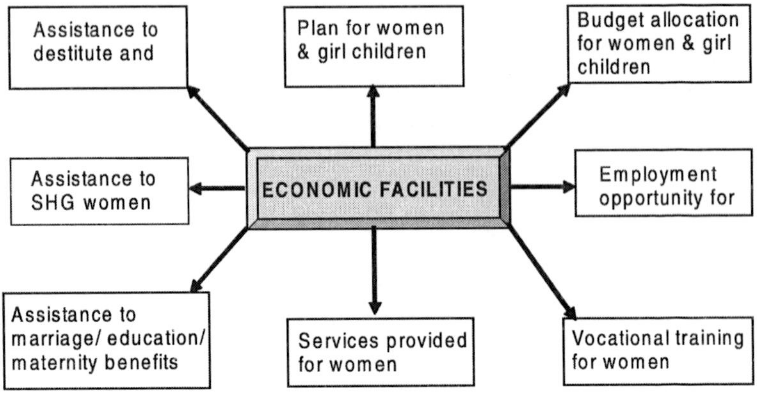

Fig. 5.2: Economic Facilities

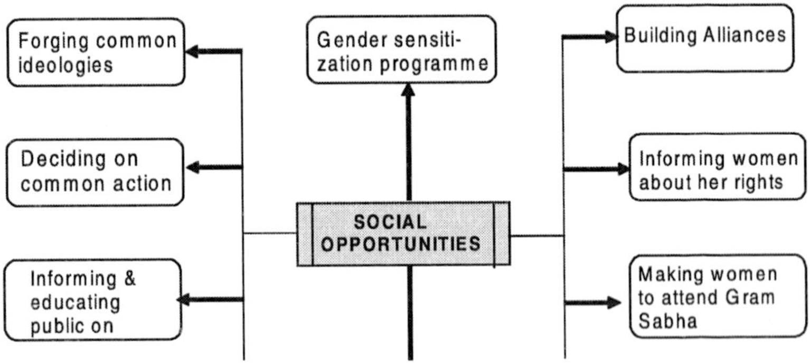

Fig. 5.3: Social Opportunities

Fig. 5.4: Transparency Guarantee

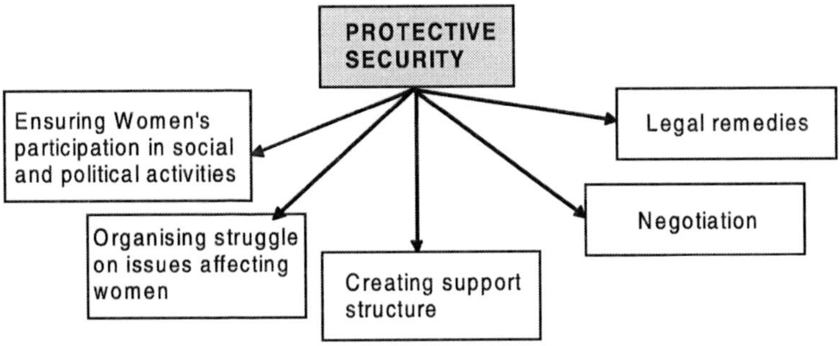

Fig. 5.5: Protective Security

Table 5.1 shows that high correlation exists between political freedom and functioning of EWRs on gender issues; economic facilities and functioning of EWRs on gender issues; social opportunities and functioning of EWRs on gender issues; transparency guarantee and functioning of EWRs on gender issues; protective security and functioning of EWRs on gender issues. While ranking the degree of relationship between the five types of freedom and functioning of EWRs on gender issues, political freedom, economic facilities, protective security and transparency guarantees occupy first, second, third, fourth and fifth place respectively.

Hence, this shows that there exists a positive relationship between freedom and functioning.

Table 5.2: Regression Between Freedom and Functioning of EWRs on Gender Issues

		R	*R Square*[a]
Model	1	.852[b]	.726
	2	.865[c]	.748
	3	.866[d]	.750
	4	.866[e]	.750
	5	.875[f]	.766

Source: Computed.

(a) For regression through the origin (the no. interrupt model), R Square measures the proportion of the variability in the dependent variable about the origin explained by regression.

(b) Predictors: Political Freedom
(c) Predictors: Political Freedom, Economic Facilities
(c) Predictors: Political Freedom, Economic Facilities, Social Opportunities
(e) Predictors: Political Freedom, Economic Facilities, Social Opportunities, Transparency Guarantees
(f) Predictors: Political Freedom, Economic Facilities, Social Opportunities, Transparency Guarantees, Protective Security.

Regression analysis shows the functional relationship between the variable and thereby provide a mechanism for prediction. Table 5.1 shows 77 per cent variation on functioning of EWRs on gender issues are explained by the different types of freedoms namely political freedom, economic faculties, social opportunities, transparency guarantee and protective security. Unaccounted for variables may contribute remaining 23 per cent.

These two analyses show that functioning of EWRs on gender issues greatly depends upon the freedom they enjoy and hence a positive relationship exist to between freedom and functioning. If the EWRs enjoy greater freedom, their functioning will be better. Hence the hypothesis is proved as the greater the freedom they enjoy, the greater the functioning they perform on gender issues.

By adopting capability approach of Amartya Sen, this study evaluates the socio-economic and political arrangements and the extent of freedom EWRs have to promote or achieve functionings they value. It examined what they are actually able to do, the range of alternatives they face while doing the function they value and make decisions that matter to them. Capability is thus primarily a reflection of the freedom to achieve valuable functionings. This study explores the relationship between freedom and functioning. The performance of EWRs on functioning is influenced directly or indirectly influenced by the freedom. These freedoms tend to contribute to the general capability of a person. This helps to look at conditions that influence women's internal development and also at conditions of the material and social environment that influence the ability to turn their ideas into action.

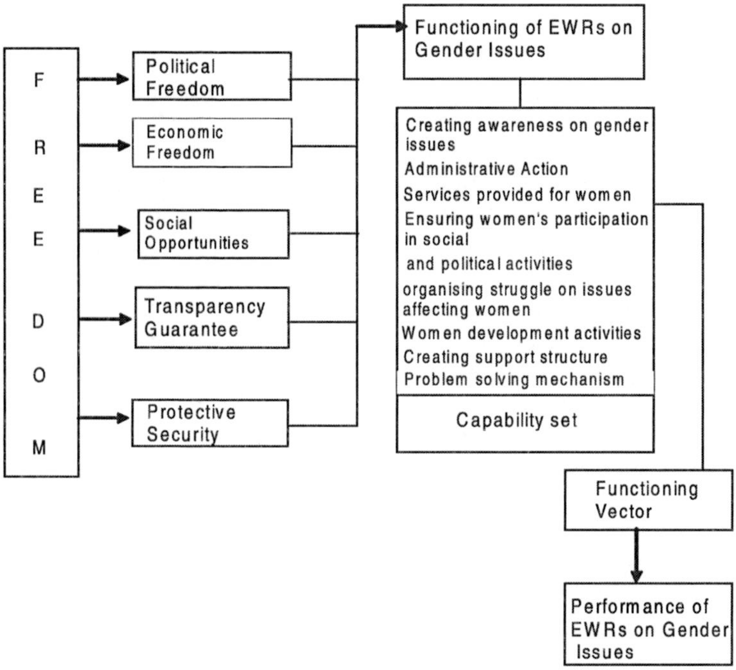

Fig. 5.6: Relationship between Freedom and Functioning

Reservation of seats for women in only the first step in ensuring that a certain number of women are involved in local government. The next step is to ensure that they have the capacity to fulfill the role and make a difference. The gendered structuration of the political space and the social arrangement need to be restructured to create an amiable and conducive environment for women to proceed further in the political path. The new meanings and the feminization of the political space are highly contested and have to again and again be negotiated and defended not only vis-a-vis state authorities and other members of the Panchayat system, but also within the village community.[4] If provided certain conditions—in the form of freedom—women in local government will make a difference as women leaders; they will bring a different style to local government and they will consciously approach the job in a different way. Many also believe that the number of women in local government will accelerate the pace of change, promote collaborative styles of leadership and decision making, broaden prospective and move communities forward.[5]

Political freedom provides the opportunity to scrutinize the political space and helps the EWRs to take measures for the welfare of women folk by administrative action, services and women development activities. Economic facilities gives opportunities that they respectively enjoy to utilize economic resources for the purpose of women and girl children development and enhancement of economic entitlement. Social opportunities support the EWRs on many functionings like creating awareness on gender issues, ensuring women's participation in social and political activities, organising struggle on issues affecting women and creating support structures. Transparency guarantee which deals with openness helps EWRs to create support structures and provide problem solving mechanisms. Finally protective security which gives social safety net will help EWRs to get legal remedies and other social support. So, to perform each and every function from the capability set, EWRs need to enjoy all types of freedom. Hence freedom and functioning are closely inter related. Freedom leads to performance of EWRs on issues affecting women. Development requires the removal of major sources of unfreedom.[6]

REFERENCES

1. Amartya Sen, *Development as Freedom,* New Delhi: Oxford University Press, 2005.
2. *Ibid.*
3. *Ibid.*
4. Stefanie Strulik, *Women-Panchayat-Electives at the interface of state and village politics: Gendered constructions of the political space,* paper for the 18th European Conference on Modern Asian Studies at Lund University, Sweden, Panel on "Gender and the local state in South Asia".
5. Jean Dreze, *Wearing a New Pattern: Women Political Leaders in Local Government,* New Zealand Research Monograph Series Paper No. 6, 1997.
6. Amartya Sen, *op.cit.*

6

Integrated Analysis

South Asia has one of the world's oldest civilizations and for its women it has meant subordination to a caste-linked, state-backed patriarchy at least 4,500 years old.[1] In Indian society, the patriarchal constructs and practices were already instituted and documented since the Vedic period. The democratization of the political system in a step by step process pushed the boundaries of the political system and allowed Indian women to exercise their rights in the public and political sphere. In Azza Karam's words "Democracy, by definition, cannot afford to be gender-blind. It must strive towards equality and representation of women and men in decision-making process and in the opportunities to achieve both these goals".[2] There are three main types of arguments supporting an increase of women in poltics.[3] First, women have the right since women have full citizenship and constitute half the population and second, women's experiences and views should have an impact on politics since women's and men's living conditions aren't identical. The third argument is that only women can take care of women's interests since men and women on certain issues have contradictory interest.

The under representation of women in politics is due to traditional norms on activities being feminine and non-feminine and public-private dichotomy where men are for public and women are for private. Men occupied the sphere of decision making for the welfare of public and women were reduced to domestic responsibilities and made reluctant to enter the public space by the norms of patriarchy. Even if there are members of government and politics within the government that support women or give particular powers to women, the basic system still benefits men over women.[4] Therefore women's citizenship and political participation remains incognito.

The representation of women in rural India through reservation of seats with constitutional sanctity came as a messianic opportunity to remove the structural barriers for women to enter the political space. While reserving seats for women in the rural local bodies constitutes a positive step for women, it is necessary to assess the extent to which this action has affected women's position in Indian society. In order to do this one must first consider carefully the nature of women's power in society, and then determine to what extent women's power in government influences the other spheres of women's lives.

Women's power and initiative can uplift the lives of all human beings-women, men and children.[5] Therefore women's power plays a crucial role in the well-being of all individuals irrespective of their sex and age. This connotes that women are no longer a passive beneficiary of the government programmes in turn indeed they are active agents who bring upliftment for the society and its transformation.

In much of India, women tend to be rather homebound and politically unassertive, but given the critical importance of political action and pressure, a real difference can be made by women taking an active role in these activities. The effectiveness of public action and expansion of social opportunities depends a great deal on the effective freedom of women to exercise their reasoned agency.[6] Therefore, the effectiveness of women's public action depends much on the opportunities and freedom enjoyed by them.

Through reservation of seats in local governance state has created an opportunity for the women to enter politics and came as a boost to women's empowerment. Several studies[7] shows that women's empowerment can positively influence the lives not only of women but also others. To achieve this state they have to come across several barriers and their capability to perform depends on their freedom.

Freedom is considered the principal means and to contribute to the general capability of any person. Evaluating the extent of freedom enjoyed by women in politics helps to analyse the following aspects:

- Factors actually assist women assimilate into the political system
- Aspects of the political structure limit women's power in politics
- Factors outside of the political sphere affect women's position of power within politics

This perspective helps to look at conditions that influence women's internal development and also at conditions of the material and social environment that influence their ability to turn their ideas into action. The present study analyses these perspectives and the analysis is presented hereunder.

The extent of women's participation in political life depends on their internal capability which is fostered through education, and external factors such as supportive social relationships. But the idea of capability requires, as well, material and institutional empowerment: the laws and customs of the nation or region are such that the woman really can go out and participate, her efforts to participate will not be thwarted by unequal legal, or financial, or physical obstacles.[8] It requires to look at the freedom which influences the opportunities of women to take part in politics and how it determines their functionings. Therefore freedom influences the capability and the acquired capability helps to perform the functionings which results in women's agency role, hence, women's agency is influenced by the extent of freedom they enjoy. This was analysed against the backdrop of Amartya Sen's capability approach. By adopting this framework the social and political arrangements where women exercise their role is analysed. Sen, classifies the freedom broadly into

- political freedom
- economic facilities
- social opportunities
- transparency guarantees
- protective security

This freedom enhances their functioning and makes women change agents. These freedoms are interlinked with each other and the analysis is made with reference to the provisions of 73rd Constitutional Amendment Act and Tamil Nadu Panchayats Act, 1994.

Political Freedom

Political freedom includes the political entitlements associated with democracies in the broadest sense.[9] Women's political entitlements in the form of voting rights as a first step were ensured only in the

20th century. Their participation in the political system has risen from tokenism to positions in decision-making. The state's affirmative action of reserving seats for women in local governance provides the occasion for celebration but they could not enjoy the freedom due to the influence of patriarchy and the climate in the government is hesitant to devolve its power to the local governance.

Women's decision-making power in the Panchayats is limited by male dominance in the domestic sphere, and also suffers due to corruption and state control, and religious and caste limitations. Women also have not attained full decision-making power within the political realm itself, even at the local level. Even though access to the decision-making position is ensured for women, control over the decision-making is exercised only at the state government's disposal. The power and responsibility entrusted to them concentrates only on infrastructure building. The mandatory functions provided to the village Panchayats in Tamil Nadu can be broadly classified as

- construction, maintenance and repairing of road, bridge, culvert, roadways and cross ways
- lighting up public road and built up areas
- construction of drainage/sewage
- provision and maintenance of public latrines
- measures for improvement of sanitary conditions
- supply of water, repairing wells and tank, pond desiltation.

The discretionary functions are:

- afforestation measures
- setting up public/private markets
- setting up slaughter house
- setting up reading rooms
- setting up recreation centre
- eviction of encroachment
- maintenance of common property resources.

The freedom for these women to address the issues of development were minimum. But when a woman, who is sensitive to the multiple needs of women holds the decision-making position, she fosters social development and also manages institutional mechanism for the effective delivery of services to women and children. They also pay equal attention to the roots of inequality which led to women being unequal partners in the society. According to the 1999 South Asia Human Development Report, some of the most basic features of a decentralized democracy should include guaranteed political autonomy and specific powers to local bodies in state, including delivery of public services, natural resource management and law and order. But in Tamil Nadu, the rural local self-governance depends upon the mercy of the state government in all their endeavour. Further they have to fight for their own place in the Panchayats vis-a-vis the patriarchal forces and also political and bureaucratic system for playing a greater role in governance.

Firstly, even though seats are reserved for women in local governance most of them contested in the election on behalf of their male family members, since men cannot contest in the election as the quota is given to women. If the quota is not allotted for women they cannot even think of contesting in the election. So, these men who could not grab the political space because of the quota made their wives, mothers and daughters Panchayat Presidents. On the one hand the quota for women does not discriminate, but there are barriers that prevent women from their fair share of the political seats. On the other hand women's significance is downgraded and minimized in a male dominated political system and they remain only proxy candidates. Even though access to political space was created, the control was still exercised by men.

Secondly, these women in local governance after entering the political arena, merely perform the functions that the central and state government entrust them to do. They implement the centre and state sponsored programmes, projects and schemes. Women in governance are expected to perform agency functions but in fact they become the agents of centre and state government. The former denotes as some one who acts and brings about change, and whose achievements can be judged in terms of her own value and objectives, whether or not we assess them, in terms of some external criteria as well. This work is particularly concerned with the agency role of the individual as a member of the public and as a participant in economic, social and political actions.[10] The latter denotes a person who is acting on some one else's behalf, and whose achievements are to be assessed in the light of some one else's goals. The powers of the central and state governments are extended through line departments and nodal agencies and these organisations view local governance especially women headed governance as their subordinates and limit their power.

Thirdly, even though elections at Village Panchayat level are free from party politics, some of the women candidates, mostly their male family members, belong to a particular political party and they are co-sponsored by those political parties at the time of election. Obviously, after getting elected they have to show their loyalty to the particular political party. But Block Panchayats and District Panchayats are not free from party politics. Sometimes the Village Panchayat has to depend on the higher tier i.e., Block and District Panchayat for performing some functions and there comes the play of party politics. Alike party men attract each other and if one is supposed to be loyal to the opposition party there comes the bloackade. Women, new entrants to politics and party politics, suffer at the hands of their family members by being proxy and also at the hands of political parties by dancing to their tune and if they belong to the opposite group they can't even perform the agent role of the higher forms of government. Political party dominance in this region also affects the women's political freedom along with male dominance and restricted functions enshrined by the state government.

After evaluating the factors above that serve to limit women's political freedom, it becomes obvious that a change in legislation requires the support and time to establish a significant form of change. Women's ability to attain and exercise power, as well as the freedom available, are essential. As explained above, the governmental structure contains gendered power relations that have been present since the creation of the system. This simply means that if women attain positions in the political sphere, they should attain the type of position that gives them the power to institute the programmes that deal with issues they feel are the most important in society and they should be able to perform functions by using their own methods. Otherwise, women's presence in government is simply reinforcing a male dominant structure.[11]

Women's political participation is a process that is evolving and developing. The road ahead is long. The actors involved in the process viz, women, society and state should be prepared always to strive to keep ahead of the changes. Giving reservation for women in decision-making positions is not sufficient and it should not be considered the end of women's political participation. It has just opened the gate for women and substantive measures are required in the discourse. Devolving power to local governance should be followed in spirit and men should opt with women to exercise their responsibilities since they differ from men's responsibilities. The women and men involved in this process should work together to be agents of change and the major share in this process lies in the hands of the state and its extent of political freedom.

Women's citizenship and political participation are well recognized, but the political environment in which they operate are not conducive and women friendly. However, women in this region have also demonstrated resilience and initiative in this unsettled environment. They have ably leveraged their flexibility and helped themselves to survive the shock of transition. The skills that women exercise at this immediate and intimate level are valuable building blocks for their increased participation in political life. Women's responsibility in terms of functioning for the welfare of women have often been put on the frontline but parallel to this expectation they are not given political freedom. So transforming and appropriating the political space is the urgent requirement. Political freedom in the form of state's prescription enforced by government, supportive bureaucrats and a range of different political actors have to help the transformation into a political space advantageous for women.

Economic Facilities

Economic facilities refer to the opportunities that individuals enjoy to utilize economic resources for the purpose of consumption, or production, or exchange.[12] The 1999 South Asia Human Development Report stated that the features of decentralized democracy should include providing local bodies with the power of tax collection upto a specified percentage and devolving a certain portion of national and state revenues to them. Women Panchayat leaders in Tamil Nadu have been lamenting on the paucity of funds available at their level to fulfill their responsibilities.

Article 243G of the Constitution clearly states that the legislature of the state may, by law, endow the Panchayats with such powers etc. Taking advantage of the word "may" in the said Article, the state government considered that giving authority to the Panchayats is purely the discretion of the state government and it is not a constitutional mandate. In this context it is pertinent to note that the observation of the National Commission to review the working of the constitution set out in Chapter IX of its report as below, as has been quoted in "*Renga Reddy District Sarpanch Association vs.*

Government of Andhra Pradesh, quoted 2004 (1) ALT659 (L.B) (Para 54)":

"The National Commission to review the working of the constitution, as part of its study, took up an analysis of decentralization and devolution of powers to Panchayats. The Commission's report records that the union and state governments constitutes to exercise powers in planning and the Panchayats do not enjoy autonomy — financial or administrative — as institutions of local self-government. The commission examined whether there has been devolution of powers and responsibility to Panchayats, inter alia in functional and financial spheres.

The report records that Panchayats, having blossomed into institutions of self-government, have been reduced to an implementing arm of the state government. On the financial domain the report observes, that to be an institution of self-government, a Panchayat should, as far as possible, be a viable and manageable unit. It should be capable of generating internal resources by using its own fiscal powers that included it is taxing power commensurate with the functions assigned to it. The commission felt that major fiscal restructuring and financial resources are necessary to enable the Panchayats to function as viable local self-governing institutions. With regard to personnel of Panchayati Raj Institutions, the report records that an institution of self-government must have the power to recruit and control the officers and other employees required for managing its functions. The constitution is totally silent about this viability aspect of institutional autonomy. The failure to address the human resource issues has definitely affected the growth of Panchayats as self-governing institutions.

The report also points out that since the task of assigning functions to the Panchayats has been given to the state legislature, state governments retain the powers of the Panchayats with state government. The conclusion of commission in this area is that the gap between the constitutional hope and the reality in the area of empowerment of Panchayati Raj Institutions was on account of the inconclusiveness of the text. It recommended amendments to the provisions of Part-IX and Schedule VII of the Constitution, among other provisions".

The Tamil Nadu Panchayats Act, 1994 has not provided any economic facility to Village Panchayats. Further the accounting procedures are very complicated and women are not used to this kind of strenuous procedure. Women manage the budget of their homes effectively. But the complicated rules and regulations, procedures, and the stringent income make them helpless. Under the rules relating to execution of works issued in G.O.Ms.No.286 R.D. dated 31.12.1998, Village Panchayats can accord administrative sanction only to estimates upto Rs.1 lakh. Any estimate beyond the above limit has to be sent to the District Collector for administrative sanction. If the estimate is beyond Rs.3 lakhs it has to be sent to the Director of Rural Development for approval. Even simple works like black topping roads up to 1 km will cost more than 3 lakhs. So practically the functions of the Panchayat are crippled.

Women have to primarily concentrate on the obligatory functions entrusted to them and the lack of economic facilities serves as an obstacle. Moreover, their budget estimate of Rs.1 lakh per annum contributes mainly to the maintenance of physical infrastructure and budget allocation for women component remains invisible. Their access and control over economic facility is very much restricted. In spite of this condition, six women Village Panchayat Presidents of Dindigul District have prepared village development plan including women component. The paradox is that, while women show their will and inclination towards development of women and want to solve the issues affecting women the way is blocked by the state government by not giving the required economic facilities.

Further, the common property and natural resources in the Village Panchayat area which tend to yield considerable income to the Panchayat are encroached upon. Even risking their life these women have to fight against the encroachment which is dominated by men. This twin hurdle cripples the position of women in governance and they have to struggle hard to overcome this. However, without the handholding support of the government this is not possible. Many rules issued under the Tamil Nadu Panchayats Act 1994 are not positive towards Panchayats. To cite an instance, the state government, in G.O.Ms.No.108, RD dated 28.03.2001, issued the "Tamil Nadu Panchayats (Determination of claim to trees growing on public roads and other property vesting in or belonging to Village Panchayats) Rules 2001", wherein certain provisions of the rules are obnoxious and do not stand to reason. In rule 7 of the above said rules it has been stated that the Village Panchayats shall have the powers to cut down or sell by auction the live trees on road margins or in water supply sources which are considered dangerous to traffic, dangerous to life or health. But certain conditions have been imposed whereby even in that situation the Panchayats can cut the trees only with the sanction of the Revenue Divisional Officer who shall accord sanction only after getting the report of the Tahsildar. Even if the Revenue Divisional Officer who is superior to the Tehsildar finds that the trees are dangerous to the public he should not give permission without getting the report of the Tahsildar. It is an unnecessary obstruction in the functioning.

The I and II State Finance Commission have given series of recommendations to devolve financial powers to local governance. But they remain on shelves and left to the discretion of state government. This attitude should be changed and the recommendations made by such constitutional bodies have to be accepted in all seriousness and implemented unless it is beyond the resources of the state government.[13] All these things have to happen so that economic facilities for better governance will be created. Better economic facilities can lead to the inclusion of gender planning and gender budgeting.

Social Opportunities

Social opportunities refer to the arrangements that society makes for education, health care and so on, which influence the individuals' substantive freedom to live better. These facilities are important not only for the conduct of private lives, but also for more effective participation in political activities.[14] Women Village Panchayat Presidents' education, physical mobility, training, awareness on issues affecting women, negotiating power within the family, help from the family members will certainly influence their functioning. But social opportunities are restricted to women, which results in difficulty which stems from the following:

- inability to articulate
- lack of self-esteem and confidence
- lack of information
- restricted physical mobility
- partriarchical controls
- double burden of work
- corrupt system
- lacunae in laws relating to Panchayati Raj Institutions
- no freedom for decision-making.

But they know what are the factors which improve them and what supports, inputs and services they need to go ahead.[15] They felt the following need for better functioning:

- The need to organise and express solidarity.
- The need for training and exposure.
- Right to information, education and economic independence.
- More of women functionaries and officials at local levels.
- Gender sensitization of elected male members and functionaries.

Education is considered one of the opportunities that plays a significant role in one's life. Similarly education for women is making political opportunities meaningful for them, and in giving them a voice once they attain a political position. One of the most helpful signs in the Indian Panchayat experience is that there seems to be increased support for the education of girls, which is likely to improve their chances of getting an opportunity to represent village interests in the Panchayat.[16] Further, periodical training, orientation and sensitization make the women leaders perform their role in a better way.

Training and capacity building are an imperative for the elected representatives of the people at all levels from grassroots to national parliament. Capacity building for the women who are new to the political space is not perceived in proper perspective and hence it is the most neglected area in governance. It not only builds the skills and managerial capacity of the women but also builds a movement for prosperity at the grassroots as the system has been created in such a way that the performance of the Panchayat can be evaluated and monitored constantly by the people. Moreover it helps them to utilize power and authority to decide on issues which affect the life of the people.

Orientation on issues affecting women and their status may help to arouse their conscience and sensitizing them on gender issues will yield a good result in improving the status of women in rural India. Through these exercises, the women leaders can be sensitized as to where they are now in terms of devolution of powers and where they have to go in consonance with the spirit of the constitutional amendment for devolution of powers and a strong people's movement can be mobilized with the initiative of the grassroots leaders. As a result women leaders can move on the right track to reach the destination.

For women, the split between the public and the private is pronouncedly informed by gendered notions of legitimate and illegitimate social behaviour.[17] This notion restricts their physical mobility and negotiating power within and outside the family and has consequences for women's independence and entry into public spaces. Its implications for women as political actors are debilitating. To expose oneself outside the domestic space may place one's "reputation" at risk—an argument that is also employed to blame women who are sexually harassed or assaulted while engaged in non-domestic activity, and to justify such violence.[18] These constraints on women have a direct impact on the capability for performing certain functions.

On most occasions women's power in politics is compromised when their suggestions are rejected by male family members for whom they act as proxies and by male co-members, and their efficacy brought under scrutiny because they are women. Within elected bodies men may receive the more favoured positions and duties associated with greater social power, compared with women. Where women are proxies to their male kin, they may be compelled to defer to the men, regardless of whether or not they are competent in their own right.[19] This shows the failure of the state's and the society's commitment to creating enabling environment for women to act in the political space. Social opportunities which ought to play a significant role in providing the choices for women have failed miserably and cannot hope to be effective unless concerns of women are given serious consideration. Opportunities should be made available to build their capacity, articulate their anxieties and aspirations, as well as voice the concerns of the communities with which they are linked as public decision makers and political actors.

Nehru's visionary statement on the elimination of deprivation identified 'inequality of opportunity' as one of the principal deficiencies that needed to be addressed. On the eve of the departure of the British, on the 14th August 1947, Jawaharlal Nehru declared: "Long years ago we made a tryst with destiny, and now the time comes when we shall redeem our pledge. The achievement we celebrate today is but a step, an opening of opportunity, to the great triumphs and achievements that wait us".

Nehru went on to envision "the ending of poverty and ignorance and disease and inequality of opportunity". But still his statement was a dream and the freedom which we got from the British doesn't percolate. Particularly women are deprived from all types of freedom. The recent legislative reform which has brought women to politics holds much promise, but their actual success depends on other types of public action. If these reforms are not supplemented with a more active programme of social change, they stand in some danger of leading to a proliferation of bureaucracy, patriarchy and other hierarchical dominance without any real improvement in local democracy. On the other side, if they go hand in hand with an expansion of public initiatives and social movements aimed at more widespread literacy, a stronger political organisation of disadvantaged groups, and a more vigorous challenge to social inequalities, they would represent a real opportunity to transform village politics in rural India.[20] Expanding social opportunity will lead to achievements in attaining quality life, obliterate the demarcation of social stratification and improve gender relations which will be cordial in nature.

Transparency Guarantee

In social interactions, individuals deal with one another on the basis of some presumption of what they are being offered and what they can expect to get. In this sense, the society operates on some basic presumption of trust. Transparency guarantees openness that people can expect: the freedom to deal with one another under guarantees of disclosure and lucidity. When that trust is seriously violated, the lives of many people—both direct parties and third parties—may be adversely affected by the lack of openness. Transparency guarantees can thus be an important category of instrumental freedom. These guarantees have a clear instrumental role in preventing corruption, financial irresponsibility, and underhand dealings.[21] So, transparency guarantee assures:

- absence of corruption.
- mechanism for seeking justice.
- guarantees of disclosures and lucidity.
- speedy judicial decisions.

These entitlements enable women in politics. But, in a transitional society, even though tenets of democracy are operative, still women in local governance cannot adhere to these entitlements because of the bureaucratic apathy. Corruption has extended its wings to every nook and corner of institutions of governance and is dominated by the authorities in power. When women enter the space, being naïve, they face problems in handling the demoralized condition. Panchayati Raj in many aspects has been made a contractor's Raj since most of the activities which Panchayats can perform have been contracted out and obviously corruption takes its share in it. Women are new to this and they have to toil to come out of this. The mechanism for seeking justice proceeds at snails pace and many have lost hope in it. There is no disclosure of needed information.

"Knowledge is power" is a strong injunction today. Women who have limited access to common contemporary office facilities are at a disadvantaged position in today's political world and this leads to deprivation of their capacity and efficiency. Most of the government transactions are not transparent and this screens the ability of women to understand the proceedings. The general distrust of state institutions such as the police and legal courts may also push women out of availing of help from these institutions. The need of the hour is to rethink the credibility of these institutions. If they continue to perform in this way it will finally affect the development of the nation.

Protective Security

Protective security provides the safety net arrangement for protection from extreme deprivation. The legal system in democratic governance provides security to all its citizens. But women, generally, do not have confidence in legal systems that throw up obstacles to progressive reforms, that typically involve long delays between charge and trial, and that do not incorporate women friendly approaches in the process of law-making. Most citizens, both women and men, experience constraints in accessing the state's justice system, marked by chronic delays in judicial processes.[22] So women have to look for an alternative institution which protects their interests. Women have now started organizing themselves to create awareness among women and to work for the development of women through different strategies, organizations, associations and institutions. Sensitized and conscientised women leaders are keen on creating awareness among the women about their problems and the remedies for the same. In Tamil Nadu, women leaders in local bodies at the Village Panchayat level have formed an association of Elected Women Representatives to sort out their issues and to have a sense of unity which gives them protective security. They have formed associations locally at block or district levels. The women leaders use them as platforms to meet the officials collectively to represent their problems and get them redressed.

They organised several meetings in several places with the help of non-governmental organizations. They met political party leaders and officials for presenting their charter of demands. They used to meet the press periodically and express their opinions on vital issues which affect the life of the people, particularly women, children and *Dalits*. Women leaders who are in this federating arrangement are highly sensitized on the issues of social development and more specifically on the issues of women and children.

As they attend periodical meetings of the federation, the restrictions imposed on them have been gradually removed. Their physical mobility is increasing without the assistance of the males of their family. Further their communicative ability has improved. Their bargaining capacity has been enhanced to strike a deal with officials, MLAs and MPs for the benefit of the people. The feeling of isolation that prevailed among the Elected Women Representatives has gone as they meet frequently. When the Elected Women Representatives face problems in administration, the federation leaders take the issue to the District Collector and to the level of the Director of Rural Development. They get their problems redressed, failing which they go to court and get suitable legal remedy which has raised the morale of the women leaders. Frequent sharing has built up the idea that this kind of exercise is necessary for their success.

Elected Women Representatives in grassroots governance are of different categories. They are educated, uneducated, highly sophisticated, rich, poor, wage earners, *Dalits* and others. There are leaders with political orientation and party background. They look at issues only from their party perspective. There are leaders without any political background but under the clutches of their husbands or other males of their families. There are leaders who have commitments and values but no awareness and information. It is to be noted that the leaders who are deeply committed to the issues of the people without political background continue to be active members of the federation. The federation attracts more number of Village Panchayat Presidents as it is freed from the party fold and the problems focused on in the Federation are mostly the problems faced by the Village Panchayat women leaders.

One layer of Elected Women Representatives is alert and they are oriented and conscientised but the other segments are not so well oriented. When oriented and motivated leaders take up development issues, they face a volley of problems. To tackle all these problems they require a support structure and protective security. They demand periodical sensitization on vital issues affecting women and other marginalized groups. They require periodical update on government orders and new schemes of the government. They are in need of periodical interface programmes. The Federation of Elected Women Representatives does not include all the women leaders of rural and urban local bodies. Those who have come out despite obstacles and barriers and those who are struggling with determination have joined together. A large number of elected representatives have not come out of their houses and have not even visited their offices. The Federation is slowly moving towards them. Even now some women leaders are asked to remain inside their houses and the males of their families operate their offices. The group activities have developed a positive attitude among the women leaders to strive for achievement.[23]

This micro initiative in institutionalizing the Panchayati Raj System, especially for women, is significant. They impart necessary skill and capacities and protect them at the time of turbulence. Given the nature of interventions of networks and associations of Elected Women Representatives it is also important for realization of the full potential of these initiatives, to building ties with the feminist movement and attempt to engender governance of Panchayats.[24] These kinds of networks and associations will really help women to enhance their capacity and moral support to take the lead in their path.

Functioning of Elected Women Representatives

Research on "Women in Local Governance in Asia and the Pacific: A Comparative Analysis of Thirteen Countries" has found that women in local government believe they make a difference as women leaders; they bring a different style to local government; and they consciously approach the job in a different way. Many also believe that increasing the number of women in local government will "accelerate the pace of change, promote collaborative styles of leadership and decision-making, broaden perspectives and move communities forward"[25].

Women have a strong focus on women's issues in their goals of local government, suggesting that changes in local politics will lead to changes in society, less discrimination against women and greater flexibility in work and child care. By bringing a grassroots perspective to local government, women make it more people oriented, and closer to the community it serves. If they are oriented, sensitized and enjoy greater freedom their functioning on issues affecting women will be entirely different from that of men who work on traditional activities like building and construction of roads etc. Women's work for the betterment of their fellow beings, in this study, is classified as

1. Creating awareness on gender issues,
2. Administrative action,
3. Services provided for women,
4. Ensuring women's participation in social and political activities,
5. Organising struggle on issues affecting women,
6. Women development activities,
7. Creating support structure, and
8. Problem solving mechanism.

Women give importance to issues that men find trivial, such as family and marriage disputes and dowry problems. They also feel the work from their heart as their own experiences help them understand the causes and nature of gender discrimination. The question before them is whether they can take up the issues immediately, because they cannot stand on their own, since they don't have political freedom and social opportunities. Further the governments, which passed several laws in parliament and state legislatures have not implemented the same in letter and spirit, which means that governments are not having the needed will. Even the agenda for the Gram Sabha will be fixed only by the government agency. The Gram Sabha is considered the people's forum but indeed the topic for discussion is fixed by the government agency and this is considered a severe blow to the decentralized democratic governance where people are at the centre stage. In spite of this, women are more concerned with social issues such as health services, poverty alleviation and community development. They also tend to work out the details and aim to achieve consensus on specific policies and programmes rather than on political issues.

Elected Women Representatives, who function for the welfare of women are models to be emulated. It is a strong notion among development organisations and women activist groups who have rich experience with women that women will bring in new ideas, nuances, energy, enthusiasm and approach to governance and that hitherto unutilized potentials will be used.[26] They have different set of skills and they enhance the leadership qualities of others. Women have developed skills to carry out works despite the limited resources and differences of opinion with their family members. Working in adverse circumstances is not new to them. Further they have patience to listen to others which men do not have.

On many occasions women leaders are honest and accurate in presenting issues to the decision making authorities. They are pathfinders in attacking social issues. Several of the problems need to be attended to for which no power is needed. Women leaders who have a service orientation in their attitudes and behaviour assume responsibilities and carry out activities in society and they become role models and they are able to set new agendas and perhaps create new styles of leadership.[27] These women have started re-examining their lives and their fellow beings critically and collectively. But this doesn't happen suddenly as soon as a woman holds the decision-making position. The women who are sensitized towards the women issues and who tackle those issues through their performance face hardship from the patriarchal society in the form of:

(i) oppression
(ii) dominance of male members
(iii) officials' dominance
(iv) household chores
(v) agitation against them
(vi) character assassination
(vii) lack of cooperation from co-male members
(viii) threat for life.

However, women in local governance have the ability to perceive the problem of their fellow beings. They have the capability to influence the process of governance in favour of women to bring about substantial change in their life. The action taken by women leaders in spite of their limited freedom shows their earnest measures which try to address the gender disparity in education, health and employment. The Tamil Nadu Panchayats Act 1994, as mentioned already, confined the activities of the Village Panchayat to providing infrastructure facilities. But these women leaders have taken many steps to curb the menace of gender disparity. Their functioning can be noted as in the following:

- Informing and educating the public about the ill effects of gender and related issues through folk arts/ pamphlets/ notices/ rally/ hoardings.
- Conducting gender sensitization programmes
- Informing women about her rights
- Passing resolution in the Gram Sabha to eradicate gender disparity
- Establishing a committee for women
- Plan preparation for women and girl children development
- Involving people in the activities for the welfare of women
- Providing services for women in the form of
  - water facilities
  - health care
  - sanitation
  - action against liquor
  - action against atrocities on women
- To ensure the participation of women in social and political activities they have taken a series of measure by
  - making them attend the Gram Sabha
  - making them participate in the activities of the Panchayat
- Organised struggles on issues affecting women by
  - bringing women together on issues
  - deciding on common action
  - forging common ideologies
- To enhance the status of women they have
  - approached sectoral departments for women welfare programmes
  - arranged vocational training for women
  - formed and assisted women Self-Help Groups (SHG)
  - assisted SC/ST women for their social and economic upliftment

- provided assistance for marriage, education and maternity benefits
- created employment opportunity for women
- ensured equal wages for women
- eliminated gender disparity in school education.

They have also created support structure by building alliance with Non Governmental Organisations (NGOs), Community Based Organisations (CBOs), SHGs and other women organisations. The Elected Women Representatives Federation has helped them a lot during the time of crisis and-mostly all the women leaders are part of the Federation. This Federation, as victory to the collective action has achieved the following:

1. Extension of reservation of seats for women for one more term without rotating the seats every five years (The local body election which was conducted in 1996 and 2001 didn't have rotation. The constituencies which were reserved for women in 1996 continued in 2001also).
2. Eradication of cheap liquor.
3. Government programmes are drafted with the support of elected women representatives.
4. Hike in central government scheme fund.
5. Rescue of women leaders from section 205 of Tamil Nadu Panchayats Act 1994 (*By using this section, the Inspector of Panchayat in Tamil Nadu i.e., District Collector, takes action against the leaders by removing the power of signing the cheque and so on).
6. The government issued an order to district and state higher officials to convene periodical meeting with women leaders to sort out their problems.
7. Interface with traditional Panchayat leaders to settle many of the issues.

These women are united together and through their collective action they are trying to ascertain their need where government has failed to take action. They are emerging as a movement and, in course of time, this movement will sweep the dirty politics of power game where women have so for remained incognito. They have begun to show their power and their voices have started being heard. This movement provides an example of a decentralized effort to empower women in Indian society. This type of approach promotes long-term change since it is based on a wider understanding of the power relationships that women face outside of the political sphere. Centralized approaches to creating change for women are limited because they generally do not affect the moral and cultural values that have forwarded women's disempowerment.[28]

Their functioning is largely embroiled by the structural handicaps which have so far kept women out of politics. Female presence in the political institutions is fundamental in a functioning democracy and the 73rd Amendment has brought substantial numbers of women into the political sphere. They, to a great degree, fight corruption, gender biases and try to involve villagers in the political process. They have brought their experiences of the private sphere and household management into the public sphere.

During their time in office women have gained an understanding of public functions and have also started to share knowledge with women in the community. All this has led to an empowerment process. Apart from this there are many areas that need to be addressed before the goal of gender equality can be reached in the rural areas. This study clearly shows that, if women are to perform their functioning on issues which affect women they ought to enjoy the freedom as mentioned by Amartya Sen like political freedom, economic facilities, social opportunities, transparency guarantees and protective security. These freedoms have considerable impact on the functioning of elected women representatives. To attain these freedoms, state, civil society organisations, family structure should join hands with women, since without their support women cannot stand alone in the battle of solving issues affecting women. The responsibility of women should be backed by these institutions and this will help to change the women's status in society.

Women's Agency and Challenges

World-wide, women's historic exclusion from the hierarchical structures of the state may have directed them to exercising their agency in spheres of influence rather than in public potential arena.[29] In India also, women's political participation in local governance has led to perceiving women's political leadership as different from that of men. Devaki Jain remarks on the recent Panchayati Raj revolution thus: "Some of the ways in which women, through Panchayati Raj Institutions are changing governance are evident in the issues they choose to tackle: water, alcohol abuse, education, health, and domestic violence. Women also express different values. Women value proximity, whether it be to a drinking water source, a fuel source, a crèche, a health centre, a court of justice or an office of administration.

The enormous expansion of women in decentralized governance structures has highlighted the advantage of proximity, namely the redress of grievance and most important of all, the ability to mobilize struggle at a local level where it is most meaningful...".[30] The vast differences in the role assigned to them by the Tamil Nadu Panchayat Act 1994, and the role assumed by them for the welfare of women folk in particular manifests their preference of action and their commitment towards the society. In the villages women begin to see themselves as more than mothers and wives, and become active members of the Panchayat.[31] But when women lack certain freedoms, viz., political freedom, economic facilities, social opportunities, protective security and transparency guarantee, it amounts to the deprivation of women's effective agency. But it is also the case that the limited role of women's active agency seriously afflicts the lives of all people—men as well as women, children as well as adults. While there is every reason not to slacken the concern about women's well-being and ill-being, and to continue to pay attention to the sufferings and deprivations of women, there is also an urgent and basic necessity, particularly at this time, to take an agent oriented approach to women's agenda.[32] In spite of the non supportive political and social climate women's independent voice and agency have initiated change at the grassroots level.

Recent indicators of women's agency range from raising consciousness of women's issues to changing institutional structures and processes and influencing the governance discourse itself. Even though the expectations on women politicians are higher, they do not necessarily do so and cannot, because they do not have equal access and control with men to the means for political participation. Moreover, the powers and functions entrusted to them in the local governance are not much significant to operate women's agenda. Also they face numerous problems when they are in power. The analysis shows that instead of tackling the problems of women, the women village Panchayat Presidents have started facing a multitude of problems. But the media projects more failures than success stories. However, such representations are largely based on assumptions, not facts. As per government statistics failures comprise not more than five per cent of cases.[33] In the Indian context empowering women is a Herculian task as social and cultural moorings have established strong roots in the belief system of the people. Their problems probably arise from the curbs on their freedom in the form of:

- increased workload
- domination of males
- negative attitude of officials and ill-treatment
- information blockade
- domination of caste
- lack of communication skill
- poverty
- interference of MPs and MLAs
- lack of managerial skills
- social cleavage
- lack of motivation
- caste discrimination and marginalization of Dalit women
- non cooperation of police
- neglect of vital issues in training
- no support base.

These factors significantly make their impact on the women's agency. In spite of this, it is recognized that grassroots women are redefining governance and development in their orbit of action. However backward they are, they want to achieve something in life when an opportunity is given. They convert challenges into opportunities, assume responsibilities and attempt innovations.

Gender inequality and women's issues do not decline automatically without proper representation from women in the political space and stimulating the process of women's empowerment is an essential requirement. Women's emancipation through political organisation and related means tends to have quite a strong impact on the unjust society which suppresses women. Women's decisions and actions can have a profound impact on the policies the government decides to pursue and the lives that people can lead.[34] They work for basic social change and therefore the importance of human agency and participation in development applies particularly to women. In order to exercise their reasoned agency, they need expanded social opportunities, more political freedom, better economic facilities, protective security and transparency guarantee.

The voices of women are not fully represented in the political arena even after one million women have reached different levels within the local government system in India. They are lacking influence over public decision making even though they form a "critical mass" to ensure adequate political representation in local government. They can create a significant impact on governance but women in society do not enjoy opportunities as men.

A profound understanding of the barriers to women in politics will help to transform the present condition and this may suggest ways and means for increasing women's representation and help women to achieve what they want. The greatest opportunity for grassroots women is given through the 73rd Amendment to the Constitution of India. There is a visible gap between the perception of governance and reality. They have come to power with a lot of dreams, expectations and aspirations. They perceive the space as development space. But, in practice, it is full of barriers and obstacles.

The concepts of democracy and development have met with severe resistance in Indian society. Women are working in the governance system which is full of systemic corrupt practices. To overcome this menace they have to struggle. Hence they have to work together. On many occasions, problems are created in the society itself as caste and patriarchy strongly work together to stop democratizing the society. The lacuna is obvious with the social setup of the Indian society with the added disadvantage of the bureaucratic setup.

The institutional structures have failed to recognize women as a factor to reckon with in human development. The government has also started looking into the development of women and development through women only after women figured in the human development report of the United Nations Development Programme from 1995 through Gender Development Index (GDI) and Gender Empowerment Measures (GEM). The GDI ranks each nation upward or downward based on its record of gender equality in the core areas of life expectancy, educational attainment, and income. GEM gives a different perspective on women's programmes by focusing on women's access to economic, professional and political opportunities.[35] The measures taken by the government for the enhancement of women in politics and economy try to dismantle the patriarchal society. In the meantime, women in their new role in politics are undergoing a different experience and in governance they have begun to mark their achievement in spite of several obstacles but their number is meagre.

Indian polity has developed an authoritarian system of governance dominated by authorities and officials and this merely reflects the society wherein men tend to dominate over women and other weaker sections of the society. Women were suddenly brought into this system as a part of the development approach and both of them find it difficult to adjust with the new system. It is very difficult to gauge the performance of women amidst the conditions favouring patriarchy and the bureaucracy.

The continued absence of women's voice in governance now draws the policy makers' attention and women tend to assert themselves and have started claiming their rights. Still due consideration is yet to be given. Much more still needs to be done. Women should be capacitated in such a way that they directly influence the broader political and economic measures. Understanding governance requires that the perception of women on governance should be altered. Constraints on women within the family and society have a direct impact on their capability for public engagements. Suitable measures should be taken to eradicate these constraints and a conducive atmosphere should be created for women to perform the agency function in the public domain.

The momentum created by these women leaders in the grassroots governance has to be accelerated if the goal of gender equity and the enhancement in the status of women are to be achieved. Women representatives are designed as change agents and in order to perform their role they must be supplemented with training and support system. The ultimate objective of enhancing the quality of women's political participation is a goal that must be worked towards constantly. Political participation is a process that is evolving and developing. The actors involved in this process should be prepared always to move with changes. Both women and men should work together so that their agency functions can be well attained. The present situation is complex and the system doesn't favour women. However we ought to proceed from here and make the voices of women in governance to be heared. For women leaders to function better the following measures can be considered:

- orientation and sensitization programmes
- networking with women's organisation and more experienced women.
- Learning how to handle the media and using them to increase women's visibility
- staying informed about women's issues, by maintaining close links with the women's movement and women's organisations
- influencing the higher forms of government to include women's issues in their agenda
- revealing linkages between women's issues and all other issues
- establishing mechanism to encourage women to speak.

A decade of experience shows that women are ready to run in the race of politics and they are in the mid-way. But, their platform is not smooth and they have to face several hurdles and this should be considered by the political and social institutions because if women win the result will be enjoyed by the all sections of the society.

REFERENCES

1. Gail Omvedt, *Women in Popular Movements in India and Thailand During the Decade of Women,* Geneva: United Nations Research Institute for Social Development, 1986.
2. Azza Karam, "Introduction: Gender and Democracy — Why?" in Karam, Azza (ed.), *Women in Parliament: Beyond Numbers,* Stockholm: The International Institute for Democracy and Electoral Assistance (IDEA), 1998.
3. Drude Dahlerup, "Using quotas to increase women's political representation" in Karam, Azza (ed.), *Women in Parliament: Beyond Numbers,* Stockholm: The International Institute for Democracy and Electoral Assistance (IDEA), 1998.
4. Alexandra Geertz, *Seat Reservation for Women in Local Panchayats: An Analysis of Powers,* www.newpaltz.edu asianstudies/ nycas 2004%20UG%20prize%20 Alexandra %20 Geertz.pdf accessed on 18.07.2006
5. Amartya Sen, *The Argumentative Indian: Writings on Indian History, Culture and Identity,* London: Allen Lane an imprint of Penguin Books, 2005.
6. Jean Dreze, Amartya Sen, *India: Development and Participation,* New Delhi: Oxford University Press, 2002.

7. A more active and informed public role of women in society tends to be associated with greater pressure in the direction of expanding health care and related public services. This link has been observed in contexts as diverse as the total literacy campaign (Ghosh *et al.*, *Evaluation of Literacy Campaigns in India,* report of an independent expert group appointed by the Ministry of Human Resource Development, New Delhi: Ministry of Human Resource Development, 1994), collective action by self-employed women (Rose Kalima, *Where Women are Leaders: The SEWA Movement in India,* London: Zed Books, 1992), and the participation of women in Village Panchayats (Raghabendra Chattopadhyay and Esther Duflo, "Women's Leadership and Policy Decisions: Evidence form a Nationwide. Randomized Experiment in India", *Economic and Political Weekly,* Feb 28, 2004.
8. Martha Nussbaum, "Gender and Governance: An Introduction" in UNDP, *Essays on Gender and Governance,* New Delhi: HDRC, UNDP, 2003.
9. Amartya Sen, *Development as Freedom,* New Delhi: Oxford University Press, 2005.
10. Amartya Sen, *Inequality Reexamined,* New Delhi: Oxford University Press, 2002.
11. Alexandra, *op cit.*
12. Amartya Sen, *Development as Freedom,* New Delhi: Oxford University Press, 2005.
13. G. Palanithurai, *Status of Financial Devolution to Panchayats in Tamil Nadu,* Gandhigram: Rajiv Gandhi Chair for Panchayati Raj Studies, May, 2004.
14. Amartya Sen, *Development as Freedom,* New Delhi: Oxford University Press, 2005.
15. Devaki Jain and Sujaya, "Development Planning for and by women: over five decades of Indian experience" in G. Palanithurai (ed.) *Dynamics of New Panchayati Raj System in India,* Vol.IV, New Delhi: Concept Publishing Company, 2004.
16. Martha Nussbaum, "Gender and Governance: An Introduction" in UNDP, Essays on Gender and Governance, New Delhi: HDRC, UNDP, 2003.
17. Yasmin Tambiah, "The impact of gender inequality on governance", in UNDP, *Essays on Gender and Governance,* New Delhi: HDRC, UNDP, 2003.
18. *Ibid.*
19. Asmita Resource Centre for Women, "South India" in Yasmin Tambiah (ed.) *Women and Governance in South Asia: Re-imagining of the State,* Colombo: International Centre for Ethnic Studies, 2002.
20. Jean Dreze and Amartya Sen, *India: Economic Development and Social Opportunity,* New Delhi: Oxford University Press, 1999.
21. Amartya Sen, *Development as Freedom,* New Delhi: Oxford University Press, 2005.

22. Yasmin Tambiah, "The impact of gender inequality on governance", in UNDP, *Essays on Gender and Governance,* New Delhi: HDRC, UNDP, 2003.
23. G. Palanithurai and V.Ragupathy, *Building Alliances and Capabilities among the Elected Women Representatives of Grassroots Institutions,* Gandhigram: Rajiv Gandhi Chair for Panchayati Raj Studies, 2003.
24. Amithabh Behar and Yamini Aiyar, "Networks of Panchayat Women: Civil Society Space for Political Action", *Economic and Political Weekly,* Nov. 22, 2003.
25. Jean Drage, "Wearing a New Pattern: Women Political Leaders in Local Government", New Zealand Research Monograph Series Paper No.6, 1997.
26. G. Palanithurai, "Role of Elected Women Representatives in Evolving Alternative Governance at Grassroots", *Social Change and Development,* Vol.3, July, 2005.
27. J. Jackquitte, "Women in Power: From Tokenism to Critical Mass", *Foreign Policy,* Vol.108, 1997.
28. Leslie, J. Calaman, "Women and Movement in Politics in India", *Asian Survey,* 29.10.1989.
29. Lina Hamadeh Banarjee, "Women's Agency in Governance" in *UNDP Women's Political Participation and Good Governance: 21st Century Challenges,* New Delhi: UNDP, 2000.
30. Devaki Jain, *Panchayati Raj: Women Changing Governance,* Gender in Development Monograph Series No.5, UNDP, New York, 1996.
31. Bidyut Mohanty, *The Daughter of the 73rd Amendment Act,* New Delhi: Institute of Social Sciences, 2001.
32. Amartya Sen, *Development as Freedom,* New Delhi: Oxford University Press, 2005.
33. P. Krishnaswamy, "Women Panchayat Leaders more sinned against than sinning", *The New Indian Express,* 22nd August, 2001.
34. Jean Dreze and Amartya Sen, *India: Development and Participation,* New Delhi: Oxford University Press, 2002.
35. G. Palanithurai and J. Vanishree, *Governance: From the Perspective of Elected Women Representatives,* Gandhigram: Rajiv Gandhi Chair for Panchayati Raj Studies, August 2004.

7

Findings, Summary and Policy Prescriptions

Findings

Increasing the number of women's positions in politics opens doors for women in terms of presence and visibility. The critical mass of women has the potential to transform gender relations and issues affecting women. However, it does not guarantee it unless they have freedom in the form of political freedom, economic facilities, social opportunities, transparency guarantees and protective security. This shows that numbers alone, i.e., increasing the number of women in politics, does not indicate that the situation for women has improved. The most important thing is that certain norms, values and social practices should change. If women have to take action, and even if such women in positions of political power take action for the benefit of other women, certain changes in legislation, educational or training programmes that promote gender consciousness should take place, so that women's agency can be rendered effective.

It is very important to know that those who occupy these seats are aware of the problems that women face and are interested in creating change within the community. Perhaps this notion on women's interest will be greatly influenced by the socialization process by which patriarchy thrives and the political climate which has the tradition of treating women as subordinates. Therefore women's functioning in grassroots governance primarily reflects their freedom. Capability represents a person's freedom to achieve well being in the words of Amartya Sen. Women's capability in grassroots governance to function for the welfare of women and eradication of gender inequity greatly depends upon the freedom they enjoy. The extent of freedom enjoyed by the women Panchayat Presidents is quantified in the following:

Political Freedom

The indicators used to measure the political freedom are

(i) access to and control over political space.
(ii) access to and control over government schemes.
(iii) position held in other organisations.
(iv) support from ward members/Block Panchayat/District Panchayat.

Access to and Control Over Political Space

- 35.77 per cent of elected village Panchayat Presidents became the President of their village for second time.
- Only 16.51 per cent of elected women leaders decided to contest in the election on their own and others contest in the election was decided by their spouse, male family members, community and traditional leaders.
- Among the women leaders who were re-elected, 19.26 per cent decided on their own to contest in the election.
- If their respective constituency were not reserved for women only 11 per cent might have contested in the election.
- 19.26 per cent feel that most of their decisions taken in the Panchayat are taken on their own and the remaining said that they are mostly influenced by their family members.
- 33.02 per cent discuss the issues in governing their respective Panchayats with their spouse and family members.
- 74.31 per cent change their mind and decision taken because of the discussion with and the influence of their family members.
- 38.53 per cent felt that they are forced to take certain decisions in the administration against their will by their male family members.
- 12.84 per cent said that with the present system of governance they could not solve the problems of issues affecting women.
- 55.96 per cent of Presidents of Village Panchayat have made complaint to the officials regarding the service which they could not provide.

Access to and Control Over Government Scheme

- 82.56 per cent are aware of the various government schemes available for the welfare of the people.
- 64.22 per cent are aware of the various government schemes available for the welfare of the women especially.
- 49.54 per cent have access to avail the scheme provided by government.
- 31.19 per cent are satisfied with the general quality of services provided by central and state government for the upliftment of women.

Position held in other Organisations

- 55.96 per cent are members of Self-Help Groups of women.
- 3.66 per cent held positions in women's club.
- 71.55 per cent of the elected women leaders are member of a political party.
- 33.94 per cent said that they have the power to influence the organisation (SHG, women's club and political party) to which they belong.

Support from Ward Members/Block Panchayat/District Panchayat

- 50.45 per cent have the support from their co-members and the other two higher tier of local of governance, namely Block Panchayat and District Panchayat.
- 37.61 per cent have the support of government officers at Block or District to carry out their desired activity.

Economic Facilities

The indicators used to measure economic facilities are

(i) previous occupation
(ii) access and control over asset
(iii) management of budget at home
(iv) ability to create profitable asset in Panchayat

- 32.1 per cent of the respondents were employed before becoming Panchayat Presidents.
- 69.72 per cent of the respondents family have land or property
- 11 per cent of the respondents have ownership of the land or property.
- But only 1.83 per cent have control over the asset they owned in their name.
- 17.43 per cent of the respondents manage the income and expenditure of their home.
- 27.52 per cent of the respondents' suggestions were taken into account regarding financial matters of the family.
- 12.84 per cent of the respondents have taken action to generate extra income to their Panchayat.
- Only 9.17 per cent of the respondents said they were satisfied with the financial autonomy provided to the Panchayat.

Social Opportunities

Social opportunities available for the women Panchayat Presidents are classified hereunder:

(i) education
(ii) physical mobility
(iii) training
(iv) confidence to speak in public
(v) awareness on issues affecting women
(vi) negotiating power within family and community
(vii) existence of the vision of future
(viii) extent to which other household members help them
(ix) respect from community

- 19.26 per cent of the Panchayat Presidents faced difficulties in continuing their education.
- 96.33 per cent of the respondents have the freedom to move in and around their Village Panchayat without any chaperon.
- 84.40 per cent of the respondents have the freedom to move within their district without any chaperon.

- 28.44 per cent have gone to various places within Tamil Nadu without any chaperon.
- Only 3.66 per cent have moved around India without any chaperon.
- 90.82 per cent have attended training programmes relating to Panchayat administration.
- 10.09 per cent came to know about the gender issues and the problems which affect women specifically after the training programme.
- 43.11 per cent speak confidently before the public without any inhibition.
- 25.68 per cent of the respondents were conscious of the issues affecting women.
- 2.75 per cent of the respondents have the ability to convince their family members that women have the potentiality to transform the village community from the level of obscurity.
- 31.19 per cent have the futuristic vision either to move up the ladder of politics or to provide service to the community.
- 22.93 per cent said that they got assistance from their family members to perform household chores while they were busy with Panchayat administration.
- 41.28 per cent of the respondents felt that they earned respect from the community after becoming Panchayat President.

Transparency Guarantees

The freedom of transparency guarantees were measured by:

1. Access to information
2. Entitlement to seek redressal
    - According to 37.61 per cent of the respondents they are getting all information regarding the administration of the Panchayat.
    - 44.03 per cent of the respondents felt happy that government officials provide them assistance when they seek their help.

- 57.79 per cent of the respondents learn about current events from the media.
- 25.68 per cent of the respondents had recourse to the redressal mechanism to solve their problems.
- 18.34 per cent have made complaints against the officials who didn't give proper information regarding their functions.
- Only 10.09 per cent felt that they can get things done without giving bribe to the officials.

Protective Security

Protective security was measured by

(i) Problem and support
(ii) Legal remedies
(iii) Affiliation with other organisations

- 26.60 per cent of the respondents felt that they are free from oppression because of their sex in Village Panchayat.
- 84.41 per cent of the respondents succumb to problem of character assassination.
- 25.68 per cent felt that their ward members cooperate with them in their functioning.
- 58.71 per cent of the respondents faced threat to their life because of being a Panchayat President and taking certain actions in their respective Panchayats.
- 40.36 per cent of the respondents faced several problems from their family.
- 30.27 per cent of the respondents faced problems because of the community leaders and traditional Panchayat leaders.
- 20.18 per cent of the respondents felt that the cause of their problem was bureaucracy.
- 13.76 per cent of the women Panchayat Presidents felt that political parties played a critical role in creating problems to them.
- Only 11 per cent of the respondents sought the help of police while facing the problems.

- Only 11 per cent of the respondents felt that they can get legal remedies in solving the problems they face.
- 52.29 per cent of the respondents are the members of Elected Women Representatives' federation.
- 51.37 per cent of the respondents felt that their association with the federation can solve most of their problems.

Functioning

The functioning of EWRs on gender issues is classified under eight heads. *Firstly*, creating awareness on gender issues. 30.27 per cent of the respondents have created awareness by distributing pamphlets and notices, organising rallies, conducting folk arts programmes and installing hoardings. 21.10 per cent of the respondents organised gender sensitization programmes in their Village Panchayats. 14.67 per cent have made some arrangements to inform the women about their rights.

Secondly, administrative action taken to solve gender issues. 6.42 per cent of the respondents have passed resolutions in the Gram Sabha to eliminate gender issues from their Village Panchayat. 1.83 per cent have committees for women development activities in their Panchayat. 5.50 per cent have prepared plans for the upliftment of women and girl children. But none of them have allocated money for the development of women and girl children in their annual budget.

Thirdly, services provided for women. All the respondents have provided water, health care and sanitation facilities for women under various government schemes. Apart from these, 34.86 per cent of the respondents have involved the people of their Village Panchayat for the welfare of women. 11 per cent of the respondents have taken action against the sale of liquor in their Panchayat. 34.86 per cent of the respondents have taken action against persons who torture women.

Fourthly, ensuring women's participation in social and political activities. 66.05 per cent of the respondents have involved women in the activities of the Panchayat. 17.43 per cent of the respondents have sought the help of women in their Panchayat to solve issues affecting women.

Fifthly, organising struggle on issues affecting women. 7.33 per cent of the respondents have made attempts to bring women together to address the issues affecting women. 1.83 per cent have taken collective decision with community leaders and the traditional Panchayat to solve the problem affecting women.

Sixthly, carrying out women's development activities. 16.51 per cent of the respondents approached the sectoral departments to implement women's welfare programmes in the Panchayat. 13.76 per cent of the respondents have organised vocational training for women and adolescent girls. 80.73 per cent of the respondents have assisted destitute and deserted women. 65.13 per cent of the respondents have assisted for education, marriage and maternity benefits for women through their Village Panchayat. 32.11 per cent of the respondents assisted Scheduled Caste women for their upliftment through their Village Panchayat. 14.67 per cent of the respondents have taken some measures to ensure equal wages for women. 11 per cent of the respondents have helped the Self-Help Groups of women in the activities of income generation. 62.38 per cent of the respondents have taken measures to eliminate gender disparity in school education.

Seventhly, creating support structure for their activities. 14.67 per cent of the respondents sought the help of some other organisations (NGOs) to fight against social evils. 34.86 per cent of the respondents benefited out of being a member of the Elected Women Representatives Federation.

Eighthly, the respondents' problem solving mechanism denotes that 59.63 per cent of the women Panchayat Presidents solved problems which affect the women in their Panchayat only through negotiation between the parties in dispute. Only 5.50 per cent of the women Panchayat Presidents felt that they can solve the gender issues with the power given to them.

Relationship between Freedom and Functioning

In order to know about the relationship between freedom and functioning of Elected Women Representatives correlation and regression method of statistics was used. The result was as hereunder:

- There is significant correlation between Political Freedom and Functioning of Elected Women Representatives on Gender Issues and the correlation is significant at 0.505.
- There is significant correlation between Economic Facilities

and Functioning of Elected Women Representatives on Gender Issues and the correlation is significant at 0.464.

- There is significant correlation between Protective Security and Functioning of Elected Women Representatives on Gender Issues and the correlation is significant at 0.422.
- There is significant correlation between Social Opportunities and Functioning of Elected Women Representatives on Gender Issues and the correlation is significant at 0.397.
- There is significant correlation between Transparency Guarantees and Functioning of Elected Women Representatives on Gender Issues and the correlation is significant at 0.270.
- Among the five freedoms, political freedom influences the Functioning of Elected Women Representatives primarily and Economic Facilities, Protective Security, Social Opportunities and Transparency Guarantees occupy the consecutive position respectively.

The magnitude of the relationship between freedom and functioning was outlined hereunder:

- 77per cent variation on Functioning of Elected Women Representatives on Gender Issues are explained by the different types of freedoms viz., Political Freedom, Economic Facilities, Social Opportunities, Transparency Guarantee and Protective Security. Unaccounted for variables may contribute remaining.
- The magnitude of relationship between Political Freedom and Functioning of Elected Women Representatives is higher at 0.726.
- The magnitude of relationship between Political Freedom, Economic Facilities and Functioning of Elected Women Representatives is higher at 0.748.
- The magnitude of relationship between Political Freedom, Economic Facilities, Social Opportunities and Functioning of Elected Women Representatives is higher at 0.750.
- The magnitude of relationship between Political Freedom, Economic Facilities, Social Opportunities, Transparency

Guarantee and Functioning of Elected Women Representatives is higher at 0.750.

- The magnitude of relationship between Political Freedom, Economic Facilities, Social Opportunities, Transparency Guarantee, Protective Security and Functioning of Elected Women Representatives is higher at 0.766.

The above findings show that there is significant relationship between the freedom enjoyed by the women in politics and the functioning they perform, particularly the functioning they perform for the enhancement of the status of women. Women Panchayat Presidents do not have enough political freedom, economic facilities, social opportunities, transparency guarantes and protective security to perform their functioning. The performance of the women in politics are evaluated in terms of their functions. But the factor behind the scene which influences their functioning is the freedom they enjoy in the socio-economic-political sphere.

Their capability depends upon freedom and functioning. Capability refers to a person's or group's freedom to promote or achieve valuable functionings[1]. It represents the various combinations of functionings (beings and doings) that the person can achieve. Capability is, thus, a set of vectors of functionings reflecting the person's freedom to lead one type of life or another; to choose from possible livings.[2] The vector of functionings possible for the women Panchayat Presidents to solve gender issues were classified under eight heads, viz., creating awareness on gender issues, administrative action, services provided for women, ensuring women's participation in social and political activities, organising struggle on issues affecting women, women development activities, creating support structure and problem solving mechanism. Women can choose combination of functions from this set only if they have freedom. Unless otherwise freedom is not ensured their functioning is not feasible. The findings from this study amply support this.

Summary

Decentralized governance with active role of women has been seen as a magical elixir to bring about development involving the local citizenry. Here representatives' proximity towards people is much closer. So they can understand the problem of the people better. The problem of women can be better articulated and a better solution can be found by women and the presence of grassroots governance has provided an ample scope for women representative to focus on gender issues.

By attaining a critical mass of women, the political norms and political culture can be changed. The 73rd Amendment to the Constitution of India and the provision of 33.3 per cent reservation of seats have facilitated the election of one million women to the decision making position in rural local bodies. The process of democratic decentralization in India, which is pro-women also, is expected to create a significant change in the lives of women. The critical mass of women in political life should increase the capability information of gender biased society.

The present study analysed the capability of Elected Women Representatives in solving gender issues by adopting the normative proposition of Amartya Sen's capability approach. All formulations of capability have two parts: freedom and functionings. Freedom helps to empower elected women leaders themselves for their own development and development of the community. Functioning represents the various things Elected Women Representatives may value doing for solving gender issues.

This study sketches women's presence in local governance and analyses their freedom and functioning on the issues of gender. The findings show that there is a significant positive relationship between the freedom they enjoy and the functioning they perform. If they have greater freedom, their functioning is better. Political Freedom, Economic Facilities, Social Opportunities, Transparency Guarantees and Protective Security have a significant impact on the functioning of Elected Women Representatives. But they don't enjoy the freedom.

Women's Agency

The factors which significantly curb the freedom of women in politics will make a significant impact on women's agency. Inspite of this, it is recognized that grassroots women are redefining governance and development in their orbit of action. However backward they are, they want to achieve something in life when an opportunity is given. They convert challenges into opportunities, assume responsibilities and attempt innovations. Gender inequality and women's issues do not decline automatically on its own without proper representation from women in the political space and stimulating the process of women's empowerment is essential requirement. They work for basic social change and therefore the importance of human agency and participation in development applies particularly to women. In order to exercise their reasoned agency, they need expanded social opportunities, more political freedom, better economic facilities, protective security and transparency guarantees.

Moreover the case studies show that EWRs have explicitly taken account of gender issues at all stages and in all sectors and pushed towards mainstreaming. They also represent a call for and responsibility for gender issues and seek the support of wide range of sectoral and technical departments to solve those so that women's status can be reconstructed from the present deprived position. These women have opened the doors of opportunity to determine the needs of rural women folk and they are instrumental in ensuring changes which are going to happen in the lives of rural women folk.

Policy Recommendations

The history of decentralized governance failed to concentrate on the issues affecting women and also the environment for women leaders in the local governance is not conducive enough to perform their functioning for the welfare of women. It is therefore, imperative to draw some lessons of policy implications on the basis of the present field study as well as review of various literatures on women and governance.

Political freedom has a significant influence on functioning. Even though women have the access to the political space through the reservation of seats, they do not have control over the political space which they occupy and remain as proxy to their male family members. Likewise, local governance is kept under the clutches of bureaucracy. They don't have any autonomy and they can't decide their course of action. The principle of subsidiarity[3] hold that the most local people capable of making a choice should make it. The principle of subsidiarity argues that most local agents whose identity and well-being will be affected by a choice and who are capable of making it, should do so.[4] Local Governance established through 73rd Constitutional Amendment Act doesn't provide any such opportunity and left the matter of power to the state government and state governments in turn are reluctant to devolve their power to the local governance. Therefore considerable change is required in the Tamil Nadu Panchayat Act, 1994 to make local governance function on its own.

Economic facilities are only meagre at the local governance and they tend to depend on the state and central government for the funds. With the initiation of several agencies,[5] micro level planning is getting popular in Tamil Nadu. But the centre and the state government do not give consideration for these plans with respect to the development of villagers as well as the development of women. There may be a link between the plan of state, centre and decentralized institutions. Usually, whatever plan emerges from the five year plan at the top, would ultimately trickle down to the Village Panchayat for implementation. Even though Panchayats prepared their plan, importance has not been given to them for implementation.

Different schemes have been created through different plans of the state as well as centre which have been implemented by the Panchayats. The first five year plan (1951-1955) began with the community development and onwards the centre as well as the state following the same tradition. This tradition of planning at the centre or state level has not changed in respect of the seventy-third and seventy-fourth Amendment Act which has empowered the decentralized governance and enumerated 29 subjects for planning and implementation of economic development and social justice at the grassroots level. Virtually, the Village Panchayat involves in the preparation of plan including the welfare and upliftment of women from their present condition, except their involvement in the implementation of the programme.

The number of schemes and the frequency of formulation of new schemes undermine development plan of the Panchayats and their effectiveness in the delivery of services. Even though the Panchayats prepare the village development plan, it may not be implemented by the centre or the state for lack of funds. This has come in the way of the success of decentralized governance. While the Village Panchayat, plays the role as implementing agency, the elected representatives do not build skills for formulation of plan and do not feel confidence over their duty.

It may therefore be recommended that the Village Panchayat should be freed from the centre or state control regarding plan preparation and its implementation. They might be sensitized and encouraged to prepare plans for the welfare of women and people's preference. State may transfer the fund to Village Panchayat based on the subject matter instead of scheme basis. Further, gender budgeting should be incorporated in the governing process. This gives the perspectives of women and their needs to be covered.

Another important factor to enhance the capability of elected women representatives to be considered is training. Capacity should be built to make their service more fruitful. Training facility should be enhanced for the women leaders. As soon as they assume office rigorous and serious training should be considered. Moreover, gender sensitization should be incorporated in the training process. This helps to make the women leaders to be pro-women in their administration and activities. Capacity building and gender sensitization are the primary requirement of the women leaders in the local governance. This study shows that federation of elected women representatives has made a significant change and helped a lot in the functioning of women Panchayat Presidents. Even though, it is institutionalized, they suffer due to paucity of funds. So, assistance may be provided from the government. This will enhance better governance.

Suggestions for Further Research

The following points can be considered for further research:

- The Indian state's response to the oppression of women can be described as hypocritical at its worst and schizophrenic at its best.[6] Giving the state the benefit of the doubt some issues can be analysed. Women suffer greater subordination and deprivation both at home and in society. While the state is trying to remove this jeopardy, at the same time in the name of liberalization, privatization and globalization enhancing the rigours, harshness and cruelty of a market friendly, privatizing and immoral economic order. This significantly affects the women especially at grassroots. Explorations may be done in this area.
- The measures and initiatives taken by the state to enhance the gender development index can be studied in depth. Women's autonomy is an important corollary of development in the widest sense — of enlarging women's choices and in the attainment of full personhood.[7] The role of state is very

much important in this aspect. Therefore elaborate study can be made in this area.

- Women's empowerment programme and its impact on enhancing the status of women socially, politically and economically can be studied. State while showing its benevolence have come out with umpteen number of programmes for women's empowerment. Their impact on the Indian society vis-à-vis states action can be analysed.
- Women's agency in social change can be another area of research. Women's agency functions are gaining momentum and the women entering into public space from private space is increasing. The transformatory process which changes women from patients to agents can be studied.
- Finally, much needs to be done in terms of female literacy, independent voting rights, change in the status of family and society, for women to fully participate in the public sphere. Therefore, those needs can be studied.

REFERENCES

1. Sabina Alkire, *Valuing Freedoms: Sen's Capability Approach and Poverty Reduction,* New Delhi: Oxford University Press, 2003.
2. Amartya Sen, *Inequality Reexamined,* New Delhi: Oxford University Press, 2002.
3. The principle was formulated earlier this century by German Jesuit Priests to insist "that people should not be absorbed into giant enterprises in which they are mere cogs without opportunity to act on their own initiative", quotes taken from John Finnis, *The Fundamental Ethics,* Oxford: Oxford University Press, 1983.
4. Khwaja, Asim Ijaz, "Can Good Projects Succeed in Bad Communities? Collective Action in the Himalaya", paper presented at the Annual Bank Conference on Development Economics, Washington D.C., 2 May 2001.
5. Rajiv Gandhi Chair for Panchayati Raj Studies in Gandhigram Rural University, Tamil Nadu has facilitated several Village Panchayats spread across six districts including tsunami affected area, to prepare village development plan in their respective Panchayat with the aid from the Hunger Project, New Delhi.
6. D. Bandyopadhyay, "Gender and Governance in India" *Economic and Political Weekly,* July 29, 2000.
7. Martha Nussbaum and Jonathan Glover (eds.), *Women, Culture and Development: A Study of Human Capabilities,* Oxford: Clarendon Press, 1995.

Dindigul District Profile

Dindigul district was carved out of the composite Madurai District on 15.9.1985. Dindigul, which was under the rule of the famous Muslim Monarch, Tippusultan, has a glorious past. The historical Rock Fort of this district was constructed by the famous Naik King Muthukrishnappa Naicker. This district is bound by Erode, Coimbatore, Karur and Trichy Districts on the North, by Sivaganga and Tiruchi District on the East, by Madurai district on the South and by Theni and Coimbatore Districts and Kerala State on the West. It is spread over on area of 6266.64 sq. km. It comprises of 3 Revenue Divisions, 7 Taluks and 14 Panchayat Unions. According to 2001 Census, its population is 19,23,014

District	Area (sq. km)	Population								
		Total			Rural			Urban		
		Total	Male	Female	Total	Male	Female	Total	Male	Female
Dindigul	6058	19,23,014	9,68,137	9,54,877	12,49,762	6,29,073	6,20,689	6,73,252	3,39,064	3,34,188

Source: Statistical Handbook 2005,Department of Economics and Statistics, Government of Tamil Nadu.

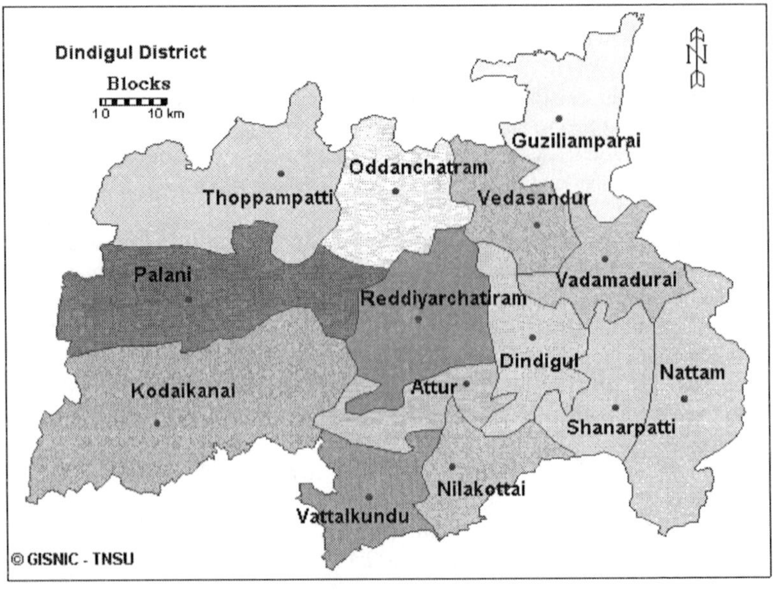

DISTRICT PROFILE AT A GLANCE

Main Workers	1991	2001
Total Workers	8,32,493	9,72,775
Male Workers	5,29,891	5,87,667
Female Workers	3,02,602	3,85,108
Rural Workers	7,07,218	7,00,216
Urban Workers	1,25,275	2,72,559
Cultivators	2,16,559	1,95,651
Agricultural Labourers	3,66,338	4,11,304
Household Industry	18,655	26,989
Other Workers	2,30,941	20,273
Marginal Workers	32,277	1,32,558
Non-Workers	8,95,831	9,46,185
TEMPERATURE (in Celsius)	Maximum	Minimum
Plains	38.1	31.3
Hill Stations	22.9	7.1
RAINFALL (in mm)	Normal	Actual
North East Monsoon	432.4	305.7
South West Monsoon	270.8	197.8

<table>
<tr><td colspan="4">AGRICULTURE</td></tr>
<tr><td>Total Cultivated Area (Hec.)</td><td colspan="3">2,27,900</td></tr>
<tr><td>Net Area Sown (Hec.)</td><td colspan="3">2,20,550</td></tr>
<tr><td>Area Sown more than once (Hec.)</td><td colspan="3">7,350</td></tr>
<tr><td>Area and Production of Principal Crops</td><td>Area (Hec.) in '000'</td><td colspan="2">Production '000' (Tonnes)</td></tr>
<tr><td>Rice</td><td>16,106</td><td colspan="2">77.7</td></tr>
<tr><td>Millets and Other Cereals</td><td>69,152</td><td colspan="2">77.6</td></tr>
<tr><td>Pulses</td><td>26,861</td><td colspan="2">5.3</td></tr>
<tr><td>Sugarcane (Gur)</td><td>7,437</td><td colspan="2">743.7</td></tr>
<tr><td>Groundnut</td><td>12,476</td><td colspan="2">33.0</td></tr>
<tr><td>Gingelly</td><td>1,964</td><td colspan="2">1.3</td></tr>
<tr><td>Cotton (BL)</td><td>4,092</td><td colspan="2">1.2</td></tr>
<tr><td>Agricultural Land Holdings</td><td>Holdings Hec</td><td>Area Hec</td><td>Average Size of Holdings</td></tr>
<tr><td></td><td>3,27,560</td><td>3,66,805</td><td>1.12.0</td></tr>
</table>

IRRIGATION	
I. Net Area Irrigated by (Hec.)	
(a) Government Canals	3,360
(b) Private Canals	--
(c) Tanks	6,185
(d) Tube Wells	682
(e) Other Wells	70,497
(f) Other Sources	1,158
Total Net Area Irrigated	81,882
II. Gross Area Irrigated	89,232
ANIMAL HUSBANDRY	
I. Veterinary Institutions	
(a) Veterinary Hospitals	5
(b) Veterinary Dispensaries	29
(c) Clinician Centres	1
II. Poultry Development	
(a) Chicks produced in hatcheries (Lakh Nos)	4.82
(b) Birds sold for breeding (Lakh Nos.)	--
(c) Birds sold for table (Lakh Nos.)	4.82

III. Livestock Census (Poultry Population)	
(a) Cattle	2,03,452
(b) Buffaloes	2,95,943
(c) Sheep	2,37,915
(d) Goat	1,78,441
(e) Poultry	6,33,371
DAIRY DEVELOPMENT	
a) Dairies	1
b) Milk Chilling Plants	3
c) Milk Production s (Lakh Litres)	
(i) Flush Season	60.62
(ii) Lean Season	494

FOREST	Area (Hec.)
(a) Reserved Forests	84,565
(b) Unclassed Forests	135.88
(c) Reserved Lands	19,730

MODERN MEDICINE	
(a) No.of Hospitals	14
(b) Primary Health Centres	48
(c) Health Sub Centres	312
(d) Beds in Hospitals and Dispensaries	840
(e) Total Number of Doctors	272
(f) Total Number of Nurses	434
INDIAN MEDICINE	
(a) No.of Hospitals	14
(b) Primary Health Centres	14
EDUCATION	
1. Universities	2
2. Arts and Science Colleges	8
3. Engineering and Technology	5
4. Colleges for Special Education	2
5. Schools for General Education	3,226
6. Schools for Professional Education	5
TRANSPORT	
Road Length (km.)	
1. National Highways	171.00
2. State Highways	164.07
3. Corporation and Municipal Road	233.43
4. Panchayat Union and Panchayat Road	2,585.00
5. Town Panchayat and Townships Road	469.00
6. Others (Forest Roads)	452.00
Registered Motor Vehicles	
1. Commercial	9,055

2. Non-Commercial	38,649
Railway Length	
1. Route Length (km.)	
(i) Broad Gauge	66
(ii) Meter Gauge	117

2. Track Length (km.)	
(i) Broad Gauge	66
(ii) Meter Gauge	117
3. Number of Railway Stations	12
Number of Sea Ports	0
Number of Air Ports	1 Private
CO-OPERATION	
(a) Primary Land Development Banks	6
(b) Co-operative Apex Banks (TNSC)	0
(c) District Central Co-operative Banks	1
(d) Urban Banks	4
(e) Primary Agricultural Credit Societies	198
(f) Housing Co-operative Societies	25
(g) Employees Co-operative Societies	56
(h) Lift Irrigation Societies	0
(i) Weavers Co-operative Societies	42
(j) Industrial Co-operative Societies	7
(k) Khadi & Village Industries Societies	35
(l) Primary Co-operative Stores	13
(m) Co-operative Sugar Mills	0
SOCIAL WELFARE (in Nos.)	
(a) Old Age Pensioners	19,433
(b) Aid for Pregnancy	0
(c) Aid for Marriage	121
(d) Aid for Handicapped	1,111
(e) Aid for Others (Specify)	40

(f) Women Welfare Cooperative Societies	5
(g) Training Centres	0
(h) Mahalir Mandram	420
(i) Women Development Centres	1
(j) Beneficiaries	1160

Development Divisions – Dindigul Palani
Block/Panchayat Unions : 14
Village Panchayat : 306
Special Village Panchayat : 24

DIVISION	BLOCK	BLOCK NAME
Dindigul	1	Dindigul
	2	Shanarpatti
	3	Athoor
	4	Reddiarchatram
	5	Natham
	6	Nilakkottai
	7	Bathlakundu
Palani	8	Kodaikkannal
	9	Palani
	10	Oddanchatram
	11	Thoppampatti
	12	Vedasandur
	13	Vadamadurai
	14	Guziliyamparai

Bibliography

Books

Agarwal, Bina, *A Field of One's Own,* Cambridge: Cambridge University Press, 1994.

Agarwal, Bina, Jane Humphries, Ingrid Robeyns (eds), *Capabilities, Freedom and Equality: Amartya Sen's Work from a Gender Perspective,* New Delhi: Oxford University Press, 2006.

Alikhan, Mumtaz, *Scheduled Caste and their Status in India,* New Delhi: Uppal Publishing House, 1980.

Alkire, Sabina, *Valuing Freedoms: Sen's Capability Approach and Poverty Reduction,* New Delhi: Oxford University Press, 2003.

Allane, Isabelle and Jacques Verson (eds), *Gender Discriminations Among Young Children in Asia,* Pondicherry: French Institute of Pondicherry & Centre Population et Development, Department of Social Sciences, 2005.

Arulselvam, M., *Tamil Nadu Panchayats and Municipal Laws, Vol.1,* Madras: Malathi Publications, 1994.

Athreya, V.B., and K.S. Rajeswari, *Women's Participation in Panchayati Raj: A Case Study form Tamil Nadu,* Chennai: M.S. Swaminathan Research Foundation, 1998.

Bacchi, Carol le, *The Politics of Affirmative Action: Women, Equality and Category Politics,* London: Sage Publications, 2003.

Bailey, F.G., *Caste and the Economic Frontier,* Bombay: Oxford University Press, 1958.

Banu, Zenab, *Tribal Women Empowerment and Gender Issues,* New Delhi: Kanishka Publishers & Distributors, 2001.

Batliwala, Srilatha, B.K. Anitha, Anita Gurumurthy, Chandan S.Wali, *Status of Rural Women in Karnataka,* Bangalore: National Institute of Advanced Studies, 1998.

Beasley, Chris, *What is Feminism? An Introduction to Feminist Theory,* London: Sage Publications, 1999.

Beauvior, De Simone, *The Second Sex,* New York: Vintage Books, 1989.

Bell, Emma, *Emerging Issues in Gender and Development: An Overview,* Sussex: Institute of Development Studies, University of Sussex, November 2000.

Beteille, Andre, *Caste: Old and New,* Bombay: Asia Publishing House, 1969.

Bhargava, B.S., *Emerging Leadership in Panchayati Raj System: A Study in a District of Rajasthan,* Bangalore: Institute of Socio Economic Change, 1977.

Bhargava, B.S., *Grassroots Leadership: A Study of Leadership in Panchayati Raj Institutions,* New Delhi: Ashish Publishing House, 1979.

Bhasin, Kamla and Nighat Said Khan, *Some Questions on Feminism and its Relevance in South Asia,* New Delhi: Kali for Women, 2000.

Bhasin, Kamla, *Understanding Gender,* New Delhi: Kali for Women, 2000.

Bhasin, Kamla, *What is Patriarchy,* New Delhi: Kali for Women, 2000.

Dahlerup, Drude, "Using quotas to increase women's political representation", in Karam, Azza (ed), *Women in Parliament: Beyond Numbers,* Stockholm: The International Institute for Democracy and Electoral Assistance, 1998

Drage, Jean, *Women in Local Government in Asia and the Pacific: A Comparative Analysis of Thirteen Countries,* Phitsanulok: United Nations , Economic and Social Commission for Asia and the Pacific, 2001.

Dreze, Jean and Amartya Sen, *India: Development and Participation,* New Delhi: Oxford University Press, 2002.

Dreze, Jean and Amartya Sen, *India: Economic Development and Social Opportunity,* New Delhi: Oxford University Press, 1999.

Duflo, Esther, *Why Political Reservations?* MIT: Department of Economics and Poverty Action Lab, Sep 2004.

Fukuda–Parr, Sakiko and A.K.Shivakumar (eds), *Readings in Human Development: Concepts, Measures and Policies for a Development Paradigm,* New Delhi: Oxford University Press, 2004.

Ghadially, Rehana (ed), *Women in Indian Society,* New Delhi: Sage Publications, 1988.

Ghosh, B.N., *Rural Leadership and Development,* New Delhi: Mohit Publications, 1996.

Gopalan, Sarala, *A Situational Analysis of Women and Girls in Tamil Nadu,* New Delhi: National Commission for Women, 2005.

HDRC, *Decentralization in India: Challenges and Opportunities,* New Delhi: HDRC, UNDP, 2001.

Hust, Evelin, *Women's Political Representation and Empowerment in India—A Million Indiras Now?,* New Delhi: Manohar Publishers & Distributors, 2005.

Inamdar, N.R., *Functioning of Village Panchayats,* Bombay: Popular Prakashan, 1970.

IPU, *Politics: Women's Insight,* Geneva: Interparliamentary Union, 2000.

Jain, Devaki and Sujaya, "Development Planning for and by women: Over five decades of Indian experience" in G. Palanithurai (ed.) *Dynamics of New Panchayati Raj System in India,* Vol.IV, New Delhi: Concept Publishing Company, 2004.

Jain, Devaki, *Panchayati Raj: Women Changing Governance, Gender in Development* Monograph Series No.5, UNDP, New York, 1996.

John, Finnis, *The Fundamental Ethics,* Oxford: Oxford University Press, 1983.

Kabeer Naila, *Reversed Realities: Gender Hierarchies in Development Thought,* New Delhi: Kali for Women, 1994.

Kalima, Rose, *Where Women are Leaders: The SEWA Movement in India,* London: Zed Books, 1992

Kapadia, K.M., *Marriage and Family in India,* London: Oxford University Press, 1966.

Karam, Azza, "Introduction: Gender and Democracy – Why?" in Azza Karam (ed.), *Women in Parliament: Beyond Numbers,* Stockholm: The International Institute for Democracy and Electoral Assistance (IDEA), 1998.

KWIRC, *Building Budgets from Below – Enabling Women to Direct Fiscal Policy,* Bangalore: Karnataka Women's Information and Resource Centre, 2003.

Litvack, Jennie, Junaid Ahmad, Richard Bird, *Rethinking Decentralization in Developing Countries,* Washington D.C.: The World Bank, 1998.

Mahabubul Haq *Human Development Centre*, *Human Development in South Asia: The Gender Question,* Oxford University Press.

Majumdar, D.N., *et. al.*, "Inter-caste Tensions" in A.R. Desai, *Rural Sociology in India* (ed), Bombay: Popular Prakashan, 1969.

Manor, James, *The Political Economy of Decentralization,* Washington DC: The World Bank, 1997.

Mazumdar, Vina, "Women: from Equality and Empowerment" in Hiranmay Karlekar (ed), *Independent India: The First Fifty Years,* New Delhi: Oxford University Press, 1998.

Mehta, S.R., *Emerging Pattern of Rural Leadership,* New Delhi: Wiley Eastern Private Limited, 1972.

Mies, Maria, *et. al.*, *Women: The Last Colony,* New Delhi: Kali for Women, 1988.

Mohanty, Bidyut and Shashi Narayana (eds), *Women and Political Empowerment,* Bangalore: Institute of Social Sciences, 2001.

Mohanty, Bidyut, *The Daughter of the 73rd Amendment Act,* New Delhi: Institute of Social Sciences, 2001.

Murthy, Ranjani K.(ed), *Building Women's Capacities: Interventions in Gender Transformation,* New Delhi: Sage Publications, 2001.

Nagla, B.K., "Sex and Gender: Cognitive Analysis" in Abha Avasthi, A.K. Srivastava (eds), *Modernity, Feminism and Women Empowerment,* New Delhi: Rawat Publication, 2001.

Narasimhan, Sakuntala, *Empowering Women: An Alternative Strategy from Rural India,* New Delhi: Sage Publications, 1999.

Nussbaum, Martha and Jonathan Glover (eds.), *Women, Culture and Development: A Study of Human Capabilities,* Oxford: Clarendon Press, 1995.

Nussbaum, Martha C., *Human Capabilities: Women, Culture and Development,* New York: Oxford University Press, 1996.

Omvedt, Gail, *Women in Popular Movements in India and Thailand During the Decade of Women,* Geneva: United Nations Research Institute for Social Development, 1986.

Palanithurai, G. (ed), *Caste Politics and Society in Tamil Nadu,* Delhi: Kaniskha Publishers, 1994.

Palanithurai, G. and J. Vanishree, *Governance: From the Perspective of Elected Women Representatives,* Gandhigram: Rajiv Gandhi Chair for Panchayati Raj Studies, August 2004.

Palanithurai, G., and V. Ragupathy, *Functional Efficiency of Gram Sabha in Tamil Nadu,* New Delhi: Concept Publishing Company, 2005.

Palanithurai, G., and V. Ragupathy, *Building Alliances and Capabilities among the Elected Women Representatives of Grassroots Institutions,* Gandhigram: Rajiv Gandhi Chair for Panchayati Raj Studies, 2003.

Palanithurai, G., *Grassroots Democracy in Indian Society,* New Delhi: Concept Publishing Company, 2000.

Palanithurai, G., *New Panchayati Raj in Tamil Nadu* (with the Act in original), New Delhi: Concept Publishing Company, 2003.

Palanithurai, G., *Status of Financial Devolution to Panchayats in Tamil Nadu,* Gandhigram: Rajiv Gandhi Chair for Panchayati Raj Studies, May 2004.

Palanithurai, G., *Capacity Building for Local Body Leaders,* New Delhi: Concept Publishing Company, 2001.

Pandey, A.K. (ed), *Gender Equality, Development and Women Empowerment,* New Delhi: Institute of Sustainable Development, Lucknow and Anmol Publications Pvt. Ltd, 2003.

Parpart, Jane L., M. Patricia Connelly and V. Eudine Barriteau (eds), *Theoretical Perspectives on Gender and Development,* Ottawa: International Development Centre, 2000.

Parsons, Talcott, *The Social System,* New York: The Free Press of Glencoe, 1964.

Ramesh, Asha and Bharti Ali, *33.3% Reservation towards Political Empowerment,* Bangalore: Books for Change, 2001.

Rani, Celine, *Emerging Pattern of Rural Women Leadership in India,* New

Delhi: Kalpaz Publications, 2002.

Sahay, Sushama, *Women and Empowerment,* New Delhi: Discovery Publishing House, 1998.

Santha, E.K., *Political Participation of Women in Panchayati Raj: Haryana, Kerala and Tamil Nadu,* New Delhi: Institute of Social Sciences, 1999.

Saraswathi, S., *The Madras Panchayat System: A Historical Survey,* Vol.1, Delhi: Impex India, 1973;

Saxena, Kiran (ed), *Women and Politics,* New Delhi: Gyan Publishing House, 2000.

Sen, Amartya, "Capability and Well Being" in Martha Nussbaum and Amartya Sen (eds), *The Quality of Life,* New Delhi: Oxford University Press, 2000.

Sen, Amartya, *Development as Freedom,* New Delhi: Oxford University Press, 2005.

Sen, Amartya, *Inequality re-examined,* New Delhi: Oxford University Press, 2002.

Sen, Amartya, *The Argumentative India: Writings on Indian History, Culture and Identity,* London: Allen Lane an Imprint of Penguin Books, 2005.

Shah, A.M., B.S. Baviskar, E.A. Ramaswamy (eds), *Social Structure and Change: Women in Indian Society,* Vol.2, New Delhi: Sage Publications, 1992.

Singh, D.R., *Rural Leadership Among Scheduled Castes,* Allahabad: Chugh Publications, 1985.

Sridharan, Indhrani, "Practising Human Rights: A Feminist Perspective" in Chiranjivi J.Nirmal (ed), *Human Rights in India: Historical, Social and Political Perspectives,* New Delhi: Oxford University Press, 2000.

Stephen, F. and N. Rajasekaran, *Sheep and Lambs: An Empirical Study of Women in Local Self Governance in Karnataka,* Bangalore: A Search Publication, 2001.

Tambiah, Yasmin (ed.) *Women and Governance in South Asia: Re-imagining of the State,* Colombo: International Centre for Ethnic Studies, 2002.

Tong, Rose Mary, *Feminist Thought: A Comprehensive Introduction,* Sydney: Allen & Urwin, 1998.

UNDP, *Essays on Gender and Governance,* New Delhi: Human Development Resource Centre and United National Development Programme, 2003.

UNDP, *Women's Political Participation and Good Governance: 21st Century Challenges,* New Delhi: HDRC, UNDP, 2000.

UNIFEM, *Engendering Governance and Leadership: 1998 Annual Report,* New York: Scheduled Tribes.Martin's Press, 1998.

Urban Governance Toolkit Series, *Local to Local Dialogue: A Grassroots Women's Perspective on Good Governance,* Nairobi: UN-HABITAT and Huairou Commission, Sep 2004.

World Bank, *Engendering Development: Through Gender Equality in Rights, Resources, and Voice,* Oxford: A Co-publication of the World Bank and Oxford University Press, 2002.

Journals

Bahl, Vinay, "What Went Wrong With 'History from Below'", *Economic and Political Weekly,* Jan 11, 2003.

Bandopadhyay, D., "Gender and Governance in India", *Economic and Political Weekly,* July 29, 2000.

Behar, Amitabh, Yamini Aiyar, "Networks of Panchayat Women: Civil Society Space for Political Action", *Economic and Political Weekly,* Nov 22, 2003.

Beteille, Andre, "Empowerment", *Economic and Political Weekly,* March 6-13, 1999.

Chattopadhyay, Ragabendra and Esther Duflo, "Impact of Reservation in Panchayati Raj: Evidence from a Nationwide Randomized Experiment", *Economic and Political Weekly,* Feb 28, 2004.

Das, Maitreyi, "Women's Autonomy and Politics of Gender in Guyana", *Economic and Political Weekly,* June 3, 2000.

Dietrich, Gabriele, "Loss of Socialist Vision and Options before the Women's Movement", *Economic and Political Weekly,* Oct 25, 2003.

Gupta, Santosh, "Strategy for Empowerment of Women", *Indian Journal of Marketing,* Vol. XXXIII, No.6, June 2003.

Islam, Nazrul Md., "Decentralized Governance and Development: A Gandhian Vision", *Gandhi Prasang*, V(2), 2003.

Jackquette, J., "Women in Power: From Tokenism to Critical Mass", *Foreign Policy,* Fall 1997.

James, H.S., "Marriage as Status Achieving Device", *Sociology and Social Research,* 29 September-October, 1944.

Kishor, Sunita and Kamla Gupta, "Women's Empowerment in India and its States: Evidence from NEHS", *Economic and Political Weekly,* Oct 25, 2003.

Kishor, Sunita, Kamla Gupta, "Women's Empowerment in India and its States: Evidence from the NFHS" *Economic and Political Weekly,* Feb 14, 2004.

Krishnaraj, Maithreyi, "Challenges before Women's Movement in a Changing Context", *Economic and Political Weekly,* Oct 25, 2003.

Mukhopadhyay, Maitrayee, "Creating Citizens Who Demand just Governance: Gender and Development in the Twenty First Century" *Gender and Development* Vol.11, No.3, Nov, 2003.

Mukherjee, Chandan, Preet Rustagi and N.Krishnaji, "Crimes Against Women in India: Analysis of Official Statistics", *Economic and Political*

Weekly, October 27, 2001.

Pai, Sudha, "Pradhanis in New Panchayats: Field Notes from Meerut District", *Economic and Political Weekly,* May 2, 1999.

Palanithurai, G., "Role of Elected Women Representatives in Evolving Alternative Governance at Grassroots", *Social Change and Development,* Vol.3, July 2005.

Palanithurai, G., "Impediments to Empowerment of Women: Experience of Elected Women Representatives in Panchayats in Tamil Nadu", *The Indian Journal of Political Science,* Vol.63, No.1, March 2002.

Palanithurai, G., "The Genre of Women Leaders in Local Bodies: Experience from Tamil Nadu", *The Indian Journal of Public Administration,* Vol.XLVII, No.1, Jan-Mar 2001.

Palanithurai, G., "Capacity Building Exercise for Elected Representatives in Tamil Nadu", *Journal of Rural Development,* Vol.16: No:4, Oct-Dec, 1997.

Panda, Smita Mishra, "Women's Empowerment through NGO Interventions: A Framework for Assessment", *Social Change,* Vol.30, Nos.3&4, Sep-Dec, 2000.

Pande, Rohini, "Can mandated political representation increase policy influence for disadvantaged minorities? Theory and Evidence from India", *American Economic Review,* 93(4), 2003.

Patnaik, Karunakar, "Devolution of Powers to Panchayati Raj Institutions in India: An Overview", *The Grassroots Governance Journal,* Vol.1, No.2, Dec 2003.

Patnaik, N., and H.D. Laxminarayan, "Functional Politics in Village India", *Man in India,* Vol.49, No.2, August-September, 1969.

Phadke, Shilpa, "Thirty years on Women's Studies Reflects on the Women's Movement", *Economic and Political Weekly,* Oct 25, 2003.

Rajagopal, Shobhita and Kanchan Mathur, "Women's Empowerment through State Benevolence", *Economic and Political Weekly,* August 12, 2000.

Robeyns, Ingrid, "Sen's Capability Approach and Gender Inequality: Selecting Relevant Capabilities", *Feminist Economics* (2), 2003.

Roy, Anupama, "Community, Women Citizens and a Women's Politics", *Economic and Political Weekly,* April 28, 2001.

Sharma, B.R., and Manisha Gupta, "Gender Based Violence in India – A never Ending Phenomenon," *Journal of International Women's Studies,* Vol.6, No.1, No, 2004.

Sharma, Kumud, "Institutionalizing Feminist Agenda(s)", *Economic and Political Weekly,* Oct 25, 2003.

Sharma, Sumedha, "Women's ways of Governance", *Participation and Governance,* 7:19, 2000.

Singh, J.P., "Indian Democracy and Empowerment of Women", *The Indian*

Journal of Public Administration, Vol.XLVI, No.4, Oct-Dec, 2000.

Singh, Pritam and J.K. Pundir, "Women Legislators in UP: Background, Emergence and Role", *Economic and Political Weekly,* March 9, 2002.

Sonalkar, Wandana, "An Agenda of Gender Politics", *Economic and Political Weekly,* Jan 9, 1999.

Sonpar, Shobna and Ravi Kapur, "Non-Conventional Indicators: Gender Disparities under Structural Reforms", *Economic and Political Weekly,* Jan 6, 2001.

Srinivas, M.N., "The Dominant Caste in Rampura", *American Anthropologist,* Vol.61, No.1, 1959.

Suguna, B., "Women's Empowerment: Concept and Framework", *Social Welfare,* December, 2001.

Tawa, Lama-Rewal Stephanie, "Fluctuating, Ambivalent Legitimacy of Gender as a Political Category", *Economic and Political Weekly,* Apr 28, 2001.

Tucker, Veena, "Theoretical Perspectives of Women's Empowerment and the Role of NGOs", *Women's Link,* Vol.9, No.3, July-Sep, 2003.

Vahedi, Farida, "Gender Equality and Social Responsibility", Sarvodaya, Sep-Oct, 2003.

Verma, Vidhu, "Engendering Development: Limits of Feminist Theories and Justice", *Economic and Political Weekly,* Dec 4, 2004.

Reports

Asian Development Bank, *Gender and Governance Issues in Local Government: Regional Report of Technical Assistance in Bangladesh,* Nepal and Pakistan, Manila: Asian Development Bank, 2004.

Ghosh, *et. al., Evaluation of Literacy Campaigns in India,* report of an independent expert group appointed by the Ministry of Human Resource Development, New Delhi: Ministry of Human Resource Development, 1994.

Planning Commission, *National Human Development Report, 2001,* New Delhi: Planning Commission, Government of India, March 2002.

G. Palanithurai, *New Panchayati Raj System in Tamil Nadu (With the Act in Original),* New Delhi: Concept Publishing Company, 2003.

Shamin, Ishrat and Ranjana Kumari, *Gender and Local Governance: A New Discourse in Development,* Report Submitted to South Asia Network of Economic Research Institutes, Submitted by Centre for Women and Children Studies, Dhaka, Bangladesh and Centre for Social Research, New Delhi: India, Nov, 2002.

State Planning Commission, *Entrustment of Responsibilities to Panchayat Institutions,* Chennai: State Planning Commission, 1997.

The Government of Tamil Nadu, *Tamil Nadu Human Development Report,* New Delhi: Social Science Press, 2003.

The Indian Council of Social Science Research, *Status of Women in India: A Synopsis of the Report of the National Committee on the Status of Women (1971-74),* New Delhi: Allied Publishers Private Limited, 1975.

UNDP, *Human Development Report 2002,* New York: Oxford University Press, 2002.

UNDP, *Human Development Report 2006,* New York: Oxford University Press, 2006.

Others

Alexandra, Geertz, "Seat Reservation for Women in Local Panchayats: An Analysis of Powers", www.newpaltz.edu/ asian studies/nycas/2004% 20UG%20prize%20Alexandra%20Geertz.pdf downloaded on 18.07.2006

Bratton, Kathleen A., "Critical Mass Theory Revisited: The Behaviour and Success of Token Individuals in State Legislatures", paper presented at the annual meeting of the American Political Science Association, Boston Marriot Copley Place, Sheraton Boston & Hyner Convention Center, Boston, Massachusetts, August 28, 2002.

Buch, Nirmala, *Women's Experience in New Panchayats: The Emerging Leadership of Rural Women,* Occasional Paper No. 35, New Delhi: Centre for Women's Development Studies, 2000.

Calaman, Leslie, J., "Women and Movement in Politics in India", *Asian Survey,* 29th October, 1989.

Drage, Jean, *Wearing a New Pattern: Women Political Leaders in Local Government,* New Zealand Research Monograph Series Paper No.: 6, 1997.

Gandhi, M.K., *Harijan,* 26th July, 1942.

Goyal, S.K., "The Study of Scheduled Caste students of College at Eastern U.P", Research Project Sponsored by Indian Council of Social Science Research, New Delhi: 1973-74.

Grey, Sandra, "Women and Parliamentary Politics: Does Size Matter? Critical Mass and Women MPs in the New zealand House of Representatives", paper for the 51st Political Studies Association Conferences 10-12 April 2001, Manchester, United Kingdom.

Human Development Resource Centre, *Decentralization in India: Challenges and Opportunities:* Discussion Paper Series-1, New Delhi: UNDP, 2001.

Jain, L.C., "Adding Life to Years", *The Hindu,* dated 11.05.2003.

Karat, Brinda and Indu Agnihotri, "Violence Against Women", *Sixth National Conference on Women's Studies,* Mysore, May 31-June 3, 1993.

Khwaja, Asim Ijaz, "Can Good Projects Succeed in Bad Communities?

Collective Action in the Himalaya", paper presented at the Annual Bank Conference on Development Economics, Washington D.C., 2 May 2001.

Krishnaswamy, P., "Women Panchayat Leaders more sinned against than sinning" *The New Indian Express,* 22nd August, 2001.

Norris, Pippa and Joni Lovenduski, "Blair's Babes: Critical Mass Theory, Gender and Legislative Life" paper for the women and public policy weekly seminar, 1.00-2.30, Friday 28th Sep 2001, Fainsod Room, Kennedy School of Government.

Pegu, Rinku, "Putting Her Best Foot Forward", *The Hindu,* dated 04.05.2003.

Rajiv Gandhi Chair, *Manual for Leadership Training for Women,* Gandhigram: Rajiv Gandhi Chair for Panchayati Raj Studies, 2002.

Singh, Yadhav Dhan, *Grassroots Leadership –Jackhod and Deoroda – in Surajgarh Block, District Jhunjuna of Rajasthan,* M.A. Dissertation unpublished, Pilani: Department of Social Studies, B.I.T.S., 1973.

Strulik, Stefanie, "Women-Panchayat-Electives at the interface of state and village politics: Gendered constructions of the political space", paper for the 18th European Conference on Modern Asian Studies at Lund University, Sweden, Panel on "Gender and the local state in South Asia".

Studlar, Donely T., and Ian McAllister, "Does a Critical Mass Exist? A Comparative Analysis of Women's Legislative Representation – 1949-1997", paper presented at the American Political Science Association, Atlanta, GA, Sept 2-5, 1999.

United Nations, The Beijing Declaration and Platform for Action, adopted by the Forth World Conference on Women held in Beijing, China, 4-15 September, 1995.

Index